Dear Ste[...]

A letter-diary written to Stephen

by his mother

ANNE DOWNEY

ARTHUR JAMES, London

First Edition

© Anne Downey 1987

British Library Cataloguing in Publication Data
Downey, Anne
Dear Stephen
1. Bereavement — Psychological aspects
1. Title
306.8'8   BF575.G7
ISBN 0-85305-281-6

Cover design by The Creative House, Saffron Walden

Typeset and printed by
The Guernsey Press Co. Ltd., Guernsey, Channel Islands

Dear Stephen . . .

Acknowledgments

I express my thanks to my family for allowing me to write such a personal record of our experience and to my publishers for making it possible to share it with others.

Appreciation is expressed to Oxford University Press for permission to quote from Gerard Manley-Hopkins' *Haven-Heaven*.

T. S. Eliot's lines are "reprinted by permission of Faber and Faber Ltd., from *Collected Poems, 1909-1962, by T. S. Eliot.*"

The Compassionate Friends

The Compassionate Friends, referred to in the later part of the book, is a mutual support group for bereaved parents. Its office is at 6 Denmark Street, Bristol, BS1 5DQ, England, (0272 292 778).

FOREWORD

I dedicate this book to all the parents and families who are suffering the loss of a child, through suicide. More especially, I dedicate it to the mother of the child, as it is through her eyes that I tell my story.

It is not written years after the event but in the weeks and months following my son's death. It is a record of my actual feelings at the time and how I began to cope with the saddest personal loss of my life.

Suicide has a stigma attached to it and most people would prefer not to talk about it. It has touched us closely here and now. Because of our social conditioning there is a danger that we may keep the pain within us, because we feel ashamed.

I do not feel ashamed of the way in which my son died. Neither do I feel I should hide the event or make excuses for it. I could have written about it two years from now but it would not have been the record of my feelings at the time. The story has to be told as it really is, so that all of us who are suffering from this deeply painful experience will feel able to express our true emotions, and, in so doing, move out of this dark shadow into the light.

Although for us, the suicide of our child can never be forgotten, it may bring us all a little closer to understanding why young people take this final step. Hopefully, too, we may also learn that we are not personally responsible for our child making the decision that death was, for them, the only alternative.

It was the year England won the Ashes, and a man called Geldof became the saviour of the starving millions in Ethiopia. Halley's Comet returned, heralded by a massive earthquake in Mexico, and the eruption of the Colombian volcano; thousands were killed.

Hi-jacks and air disasters hit an all-time record and the death toll mounted. Children were very much in the news, and large sums were raised by telethon appeals for children in need.

It was the year Prime Minister Margaret Thatcher stirred up the Irish problem by signing an agreement with Dublin, and the year when President Reagan and the Russian leader Mr Gorbachov began to talk seriously with each other about the nuclear threat.

It was the year we had a summer without any sun.

It was the year that Stephen died.

When the wind blows, the cradle will fall,
Down will come baby, cradle and all . . .

Dear Stephen . . .

Looking through the window that August morning, I saw them carry your body out of the house, covered with a rough, brown blanket. Two strangers in black took you away.

I could not believe it was you; I wanted to die.

People filled the house. A policeman gave me the note you had left. I tried to read it but only bits of it registered; about how you were to blame because you felt you would not fit in at University; how you knew we all loved and cared for you but you could not manage to love yourself. The words began to blur and then someone took the note away and talked about inquests and evidence.

We just kept holding on to one another because we could not stand up alone. The doctor was muttering about how you could have been saved if you had chosen another way; how he could have dealt with an overdose. He seemed to go on and on — I just wanted him to go away.

No one could help us. We couldn't even help each other.

Days followed days. There were cards, flowers, telephone calls and that terrible funeral. Blank faces everywhere. My body would not function. I felt my soul had been hung out on a tree somewhere. There was no control. The funeral car moved so slowly. I got out at the church, wanting only to sit on the steps and moan. No one could help. A lady asked about hymns and I said 'Yes'. What else could I do?

I reached the front of the church somehow and sat down. I looked at the crucifix and begged for help and release from this pain. There was a hymn I sang and some prayers I repeated from the Requiem Mass. I couldn't cry any more. At the graveside I felt nothing, only your name — Stephen, Stephen.

My hat blew off as I was leaving. When I turned round, I saw your father, struggling in nettles, trying to retrieve it. Was that you, Stephen? One of your practical jokes, to show me that we had not buried you and that you were still around? So where are you, Stephen, where are you?

Two weeks went by. I cooked no food. I cleaned the house continually and repeatedly filled the washing machine with clothes. I saw you one morning, just as I was waking. You were flying, with your arms in the air and your palms facing outward. Your eyes were blazing. You looked shocked and afraid. I reached out to you and called your name but you disappeared. I will never forget that picture of you.

As the days continued, we would all get into the car and drive to anywhere and back. We would sit outside and eat, constantly talking about you. There was a desperate need to be outside, nearer to the earth. Andrew, your younger brother, went away to stay with friends and I wrote dozens of thank-you letters and asked everyone to pray for you.

I love you, Stephen; you are always with me. I am holding on to your favourite old green sweater as I read and re-read your note.

After the inquest, they reported your death in the local paper; 'Mystery Death of Clever Boy', they said. Your 'A' level results were high and your worst fears came true. You were accepted on the Biochemistry Course at University.

September

It is now September and the sun refuses to stop shining. After all those months of wind and rain, it feels like an insult. I went into the shopping centre today and saw a child press the 'Stop' button on the escalator. His mother went on and on in one of those voices I hate; loud and pretentious. She told the child repeatedly what a great disappointment he was to her, and how naughty he was. The Assistant and I agreed that the 'Stop' button was placed too low, and that young children could not help being curious. This led to an abusive verbal attack from the mother. "Listen," she said "I told him not to touch the button; he knows! Four times I told him, four times." I turned away and carried on with my shopping. As I came down the stairs there she was, still talking to someone. As I passed, she pointed an accusing finger at me and said "That's one of them". I looked at her, but no words came. I felt I was in some way on trial.

I see pictures of you in my head, Stephen. It's like a film with a constant action replay. You are walking and leaning slightly forward as you always did, your toes pointing outwards. You are laughing, always laughing. When you talk your voice is so clear. Why do I *need* you so? Without you everything is so sad, so sad and empty. As the weeks pass, there are some good short hours, better than before, but the bad times are worse, much worse. Whether it is a good or a bad moment, you never leave my head, Stephen.

I have constantly asked myself why you left us. I've blamed myself, although you said it was not because of anything any of us said or did. I have terrible physical feelings, like hailstones pouring inside of me. I wake very early in the mornings, sweating and fearful. Sometimes I wonder if it all really happened or whether I imagined it. Never in all my imaginings did I ever see you taking your own life. Not you, Stephen. You were so strong in your convictions about suicide and your opposition to what you called 'the easy way out' — although I do remember that you began your letter with those very words: "Once again I'm taking the easy way out". Why "once again"? You never took the easy way out. You always worked hard and never refused to do anything that was asked of you.

I have gone through your astrological chart and I can see that present planetary transits might lead you to seek drastic solutions to your problems. You were always a positive person. Sometimes you had feelings of great anger and then quickly became sorry. You were always saying that you made decisions without thinking things out properly then later you regretted your first decision.

I am sure you made such a hasty mistake that night, Stephen. I pray daily that you were not fighting to rectify it and could not. I pray that you just passed out.

I miss you, far, far more than even I was aware of. I just need to feel you are around somewhere, anywhere. A non-acceptance of death like this is a painful human affliction. You spoke highly of me in your letter and wanted me to conquer the world. You thought I had worked so hard for so long for so little. It is almost as though you paid some kind of price for me. I want to tell you that I do not *always* "rise above it", as you put it Stephen. I have often sunk so low, I really thought I would die. I am sure I told you that when things are black as black, some small thing happens and it all looks suddenly right again. You say you hope that I will recover; well, that remains to be seen. I know I have never been so devastated by any event in my life, nor felt such a heavy, desperate sadness. Your loss leaves a gap so wide that it will be impossible ever to fill it.

You say you want to remain with us in spirit always and would like the boys to remember you for all the laughs you had together. How could they ever *not* do so! You were envied, Stephen. Your dismissal of all things trivial, your totally non-materialistic attitude and your one-liner jokes were unbeatable. I can still hear you laughing — your laughter was so contagious. I can see you now, giving Andrew the bear hug. He has abandoned his bear collection since you left us, and somehow I feel that I will eventually have to explain to him why you felt you had to go.

I looked today at your photograph, taken two years ago when you were sixteen and a half. Such a lovely face. So young. You said your photographs were terrible. This one wasn't. You looked positive and happy and I cried. I will never really understand, Stephen. Was it my fault? Perhaps I wasn't positive enough; I should have laughed more. Sometimes I wonder what God expects of me. When I look at your face, I think eighteen years and then you are gone from us because of one drastic decision, one night. I cannot let your life mean nothing, Stephen, I just cannot.

It is now the end of September and the sun has moved into the sign of Libra. Each week I put flowers on your grave and find a certain peace in that little churchyard at the bottom of our road. You passed by it for seven years on your way to school! I am sure you never thought you would be lying there. You wanted always to be with us, Stephen, so I have arranged to have a little plaque — nothing special because I know you hate show. Your full name is on it; the day you were born, and the day you died. I have answered your request with a little inscription which says "Stephen, you are always with us". I know you are not there, actually in the grave I mean, but that is where you left us. I am sure your real self is around, watching me. Knowing you, you are probably feeling that I should not follow such maudlin practices. In fact, I can hear you say in my head "It's OK caring, Mum, so long as it does not make you unhappy". So far, someone has always come with me to the churchyard, either your father or one of your brothers.

Today Mark came, and we sat at your graveside and talked about you; what you said in your note; what you said when Mark left for Africa, about how you were going to miss him more than you thought. He felt bad because he had not replied to your letter, but he was waiting until your examination results came out so that he could congratulate you. He showed me your letter to him and as always you made me laugh when you said "Be careful — because Maharishi Mum sees that at the moment the Sun is not very well aspected to Uranus — take heed!!". You went on to apologise for your delay in writing, saying: "Two months to find a bloody pencil sharpener!". You did mention how you missed him, saying that he provided "an additional emotional crutch to lean on".

I must admit that this surprised me as I always thought you were so well sorted out with many of the problems of the teenage phase behind you. You didn't give much away, Stephen; perhaps you thought I had enough to cope with. The guilt surrounding me is almost too much to bear. There you were, making me laugh because you wanted to lighten my life and there I was accepting all from you without realising how much more you needed from me. Your letter went on to sympathise with Mark who would feel sad being away from home at Christmas because you felt Christmas was "a family affair". You pulled yourself up quickly because you felt the tone of the letter was becoming far too miserable. You talked affectionately about your father as "the Oldham

Roughhead himself" who had probably now become "The beer man of Al Khobhar"!

As always you finished with a joke; strangely, it was a joke about death. You named it "the quote of the week by Woody Allen". Ironically it went 'What is it about death that bothers me so much — probably the hours'.

I had a strange dream the other night. Since my parents died, I have dreamt of them often but they were always together in the dream. In this dream, my father was alone. I was on my knees on the floor, looking at my father who was standing very tall beside me. I was crying and did not like it where I knelt. Suddenly, he lifted me up, high above his head. I wasn't curled up but in a straight line, as though I were weightless. While he was lifting me, I shouted 'No, don't do that'. He took no notice and he never spoke. Suddenly, I felt wonderful and cried out in amazement at the beautiful warm glow I felt around me. As I was about to bask even longer in this feeling, I awoke. As you know, I am always dreaming, and often very vividly.

I recall two dreams about you, Stephen, in the year you died. The first was in January. We were walking together along a kind of boulevard and decided to sit beside a large tree and have some refreshment. It started to rain heavily and dark storm clouds gathered. We ran into a shop that had one of those tingling bells as you open the door. As we stood inside the door, I could smell incense as though we were in some kind of church. It was very quiet and I didn't like it. I was aware of someone approaching but I could not see anyone until a black hooded figure loomed in front of me. There was no face but the figure was trying to take hold of me. I started to beat the figure as hard as I could. It seemed to go on for hours, until I was completely exhausted. The figure never once tried to hit back but it would not disappear or fall down. I kept shouting at you to get out of the shop. When I turned around, you had disappeared. I awakened fearful and sweating. Thinking about this dream now, was the bell on the door a warning, the black figure death, and your disappearance your death? At the time I just took it to be a nightmare. How could I possibly associate death with such a young person, as happy-go-lucky as you?

The second dream was in April of that year. We were riding together on horseback and came face to face with a ferocious-looking animal. Before I could make out the exact species of the animal, the beast began to tear off its skin, to reveal a sheep. I turned round to look at you, and your eyes were staring. They were exactly the same eyes as the sheep.

The dream bothered me at the time because although I had often dreamt about you and Andrew together, this was the second dream I had had involving just you and me. I remember thinking that perhaps you were not what you appeared to be. Perhaps I did not want to know or could not face the fact that there was any problem. Even on the night before you died, when I was talking to you just before I went off to bed, I looked at your eyes and saw that sheep. Those eyes looked sad and slightly watery. When I walked up the stairs and said "goodnight" to you and you did not answer, I stood on the staircase for about half-a-minute, wondering whether to go on up, or go down again. You always answered when I said 'good-night'. I walked upstairs, Stephen, and I never saw you again. Now I read T. S. Eliot's poem and I am torn apart:

> *Eyes that last I saw in tears*
> *Through division*
> *Here in death's dream kingdom*
> *The golden vision reappears*
> *I see the eyes but not the tears*
> *This is my affliction.*
>
> *This is my affliction*
> *Eyes I shall not see again*

Eyes of decision
Eyes I shall not see unless
At the door of death's other kingdom
Where, as in this,
The eyes outlast a little while
A little while outlast the tears
And hold in derision.

Your best friend called today. He was leaving for University and came to say good-bye. I felt very sad, thinking that you too, Stephen, would have been going. All I could think of was you lying in a grave at the bottom of the road and the carnations I put there on Tuesday, looking sad by now. Suddenly I recalled a conversation some months ago with your brother Martin. He was talking avidly about you going to University and joining him; about the clubs on the campus you should get involved with, and the ones you should not. He was really looking forward to showing you around and giving you some of his expertise; smoothing off the rough edges for you. I see his sad face now, with much of his enthusiasm dampened, as he stands alone. I hope you are around, Stephen, and even if you come to him only in dreams, give him some solace.

Oh! this is a diabolical day. I feel so alone; lost, lost, lost.

October

The month of October trundles onwards and today is my birthday. There are many cards and presents, and the boys have even put your name on my birthday card; you are still here, Stephen. I bought a new vase for your grave and took down some flowers. Sometimes I feel you died this morning; sometimes I feel it was years ago; sometimes I feel you are

21

not dead at all. There are some very bad days when, although outwardly I appear to be in control, there is a weeping in my soul. It's not self-pity, it is more 'why *me*, why *my* son?' Everything in my life has been narrowed down to this event. There does not seem to be anything else.

November

In the Christian calendar, we have now reached the month of the Holy Souls. I dreaded its arrival. We are supposed to feel close to our loved ones who are gone from us. Not that I will ever feel any other way, but this is surely a month of tears. I feel that when *I* die, it will be in this month. Strangely, Stephen, you left us in the sunshine month of August, except that the sun did not shine that year. I am writing to you now in the dark month of November and the sun *is* shining. I have started to do the quick crosswords we used to do together and when the answer to a clue comes immediately, I hear you say "Good one". You always said that when *you* hadn't thought of the answer yourself!

Yesterday one of the answers was 'despair'. I could hardly write it down. I thought of you on that night and realised that you must have been experiencing dreadful despair, you who so often told me not to worry so. You used to make me laugh and say "Well, I blame . . ." some obscure name you thought up, and then you would laugh and I could never help but join in. Did you laugh to hide the darker side of your nature, Stephen? I feel I am guilty of the same fault, hiding my real feelings from others and doing all my own real crying alone. What a bad example I gave you! I am very quiet nowadays, in case I give out the wrong message. Just being alive is such a great responsibility. But how can we receive any help if we don't give out the signals?

The alarm is going on your watch, so it must be 11.55. You must have set it for something and I've never changed it. I keep the watch in my bag; it comforts me.

December

We are getting closer to Christmas. I feel very mixed up today; sadder than usual and, for no obvious reasons, exhausted. Your father has been home for a few days, feeling very depressed and that has added to my already low state.

I went Christmas shopping with little enthusiasm. It is amazing how I can keep occupied, cooking, cleaning, shopping and sorting out problems and yet you still never leave my thoughts. How do I manage that? Every time I get the bus home, I expect to see you because you often used to catch the same bus. How can you have gone, Stephen?

Some people tell me to let go or you will never be at peace in your afterlife. It is amazing how much appears to be known by everyone else about life after death. Why wasn't I given all this information, with all its rules and obligations? I was taught that God gave His only Son for our salvation. I have 'given' mine, but I had no choice. Does that mean that all the mothers in the world, whose sons have died, are equal to the same kind of sacrifice? Is that why the pain is so bad?

The sun now shines in Sagittarius and your birthday is approaching. I called to see the sculptor who is making the headstone for your grave. Your name blazed up at me from the grey stonework. I thought I was dreaming. What was *your* name doing there? I never imagined that I would be giving you a headstone for a birthday present!

23

My visit to your grave today was not very good. Before today, the sun had always shone, but today it is snowing hard, and the place looked so different, so sad, so final. I take flowers as a reminder of constant renewal, symbolic of the fact that we never really die. I know you understand.

There is a great heaviness hanging over me. There is also a realisation that no matter how much I wish, or how hard I concentrate, you will never come back to me in this world. I have a need to hold you so that I can rid myself of this enormous build-up inside me. I feel I am filled with heavy weights that are getting tighter and tighter. I was alone tonight, cooking the evening meal, when suddenly these great sobbing noises welled up. I feel such a failure not knowing how *you* felt. How can I help anyone else when I could not even help you?

I keep trying to think of signals you sent out, but, apart from your sad face that last night, I cannot think of any. Most of the time you were always so positive and cheerful and seemed to have everything under control. Perhaps that was it. You were too much in control. I used to wonder why you had not gone through the usual display of teenage rebellion. You were too perfect. I should have known. If only you had said you were unhappy or you had broken down in tears, we could have started from the beginning again.

I remember a discussion we once had when I ended up saying that we are all alone in the end. I should never have said that, although it is true. I was talking to you as though you were a wise old sage instead of a young man with all the confusions of youth on your shoulders.

There is a full moon tonight, and Halley's Comet is as close to us as it will ever be. I've been outside to have a look at it, but I did not see anything. There is little chance of a sighting with so bright a moon. They say mid-December will give a better view. I will look again on your birthday when there is a new moon. We talked about that, didn't we? We went into all the astrological implications for your new beginnings, back to your roots and all that.

I read in the evening paper tonight about a student found dead on a University campus. He was called Stephen. I thought about his parents and their sadness. Oh! what is it about young thinking people? Do they see no hope or alternative to finishing it all off? Do they know something we older people do not know? I remember Oscar Wilde said that too much thinking was bad for you — you could die from it!

I feel I have stepped back again, back to where I was before you left. Are you really not around any more? Did all this happen? Perhaps I dreamt it ! No — I remember it but it seems part of another time, when something terrible happened to us all. It is over now and you and I can communicate again. I realise that you will never really go and that your spirit lingers on. Somehow, we cannot leave you out; you will always be part of us. A merging has taken place and you have been brought back to us, in our minds and hearts, so that we carry you with us throughout the rest of our lives; not as a heavy burden now but as an essential part of our souls. In moments of human weakness, I see you as you were on that final night and I scream "No! No!" During such times, I feel a cool breeze around my face and I become calm. Is this your way of helping my frail humanity?

Today the sun is shining and for once I appreciate its rays. Andrew and I decorated the Christmas tree — just a small one this year. We will never have such a glorious tree as we did on your last Christmas with us. Remembering that year, when your father was in the Middle East and Mark was spending the festive season outdoors in Africa with the stars for a roof, having no job or residence, I recall my remarks. "Although we are not all here," I said, "this will be our last Christmas as a family, under this roof." I knew it would never be the same again. I did not know why or how; it was just a feeling. We took photographs of everyone eating Christmas dinner and the table was the very best we have ever had. We haven't left the house yet, Stephen, but we will not be spending Christmas at home this year.

I had another strange dream last night. There was a large house and I stood at the door, looking down a corridor to another door. I was very frightened and would not go into the house. I put some parcels inside the entrance and then turned around and walked down a lane opposite. I met a lady there and she told me she knew a young man who must live at the house. Every day she saw him in the morning going out, and in the evening coming home again. Was she talking about you, Stephen? Suddenly, I was standing on a bridge with an aunt of mine who died many years ago. I once stayed with her as a child when my mother was ill. She tried to persuade me to move onwards across the bridge but I just remained there at her side. Then I was back at the house again and I heard your father's voice calling "I'm here, I'm here". He wasn't there. There was no one there.

It is the eve of your birthday and I suddenly feel I should hang out banners for the able people in this world. You know who they are. They get on with things and appear to have no problems. When they are successful in any venture, everyone tells them how lucky they are. They usually pass examinations and get through interviews. They are the kind of people who have time to listen to your problems and never

26

tell you about their own. But they don't take up any of your time, so they are ignored. Could it be possible that they put in an enormous amount of effort which goes completely unnoticed? Surely they need a cheerleader because, without them, where would we all be? How we take them for granted and rarely bother to thank them for listening or for being just the way they are. They must feel very lost and left out as we spend precious hours and energy with the parasites who lean on us and moan and cause us so much hassle.

I heard of a young girl who worked in a group with many others. She was bright and intelligent, but the one thing that made her stand out against the rest was the amount of effort she contributed. The teacher in charge of the class was aware of this but never made any comments to the girl. One day, after class, she went up to the teacher in tears and said "Why is it you spend so much time with the people who are not in the least interested in learning and never take time out to find if I am having any problems?" "You don't need me," said the teacher, "you seem to get by admirably." "I need you not to ignore me," said the girl. "Sometimes I struggle for hours with a problem and and it would be nice occasionally to have just a little praise for the effort I put in, even if it's only 'Well done'!"

We do take for granted the people who cause us no trouble, so much so that in the end we ignore them altogether — until of course they are not there any more.

The twelfth of December. It's your birthday today, Stephen. After a week of damp darkness, the sun shone brightly and the skies were blue. Mark and I went to a Mass which was celebrated especially for you. Strangely, the chapel where the Mass was held at one time was used by the nuns from a convent nearby. Years ago, long before you were born and long before we came to live in this part of the world, my two favourite aunts took a holiday at the convent and

27

attended Mass in this same chapel. As I knelt in the bench, I thought about them having knelt there all those years ago. I'm glad they did not have to suffer the loss of you. It would have been too great a burden for them to bear.

I looked out of the window at the lovely garden, covered in autumn leaves, and thought of the day you were born; such a happy day. Your grandfather came to the hospital to visit you — and you know how he hated those places. In fact, of all the boys, you were the only one to have that privilege! You always reminded me of him; your face, manner and most of all the way you stood, with knees slightly bent and toes turned out. You had his quiet ways and dry wit. I hope he is comforting you now in that eternal heaven in which I try daily to believe.

I had to stay in hospital an extra week because the rest of the boys caught measles. I remember crying for two days because I could not go home. When we were eventually allowed out of the hospital, we received a wonderful welcome from your father and the boys. I had prepared for Christmas before your birth so there was little to do. It was a really happy time for us all. The boys had recovered and you were such a delightful baby. You just slept, ate and smiled.

This will be our first Christmas without you, Stephen, and I cannot begin to tell you what an enormous gap it leaves in our lives.

Today of all days, I was meant to sit my driving test. I actually got as far as entering the test centre. Then, about two minutes before I was due to drive out, I suddenly felt very ill. I had a blinding headache and thought I was going to faint. All I could see through the windscreen were red and white flashing lights. The instructor cancelled the test and drove me home. I fell fast asleep. I woke up crying and felt such a failure. I had let you down, Stephen. Then I thought of all the pressures upon me to pass this test. People telling me I would, not to worry and that it would be good for me to start getting on with life again.

I thought of you and the number of times you were asked when your 'A' level results were due and how you were sure to pass. I realise now what this kind of pressure can do when you are feeling so low. It gets to the stage when passing and failing seem equally bad alternatives. The pressure to succeed creates much tension and the fear of failing much despair. Better not to do either. Is that why you took your own life, just one week before the results were known? Anyway, who said you ever wanted to study Biochemistry?

I recall the dilemma you went through when you had to choose the subjects for your 'A' levels. There was no real help. Your best subject at school was always History; it was the one you enjoyed most. Because you happened to be bright and intelligent, you were steered towards the sciences, as though they were in some way superior. Between us, we had to think of a scientific subject to go with Chemistry and Mathematics and it was only by accident that I suggested Biology, because you had taken an interest in the subject when you were younger. Although you did well in Mathematics, I know you hated the subject. Martin, studying at the very University to which you would have gone, is in his final year of a Chemistry degree. It's ironic really, when we all know that his best subject is English. He is so good with words that he should probably have become a writer or a poet. Anyway, you will be very happy to know that when he has achieved his 'piece of paper', which everyone keeps telling him is essential if he wants to get a job, he is going to volunteer to help in the Third World. I know that will appeal to you. He will probably get a good degree and then tell them to stuff their system!

I wonder how many people are out there doing things expected of them by other people? You must have often wondered in the last year, Stephen, just what it was all about.

29

You had been channelled through a system which gave you no alternatives — what a dilemma!

You, Stephen, would never let anyone down. If you knew you had passed, you would have felt compelled to carry on — even though you hated the whole idea. Had you failed, you would have felt equally bad and that you had let us all down. None of us really expected anything from you and yet we did manage to pressurise you without realising it, by continually assuring you of success. What a way to go on about things, pushing able children through this charade. So you worked hard and achieved three fine 'A' levels! So what! But no one mentioned the price you might have to pay for the system they created.

People are labelled and packaged and thrown into categories. There is no real continual process; just jerks and stops along the way.

We have now reached the time of year I have dreaded since your death. The gap is even wider now. You would have been returning home after your first term with all your stories and jokes. I know you would have found something at which to laugh. Your friend called today, and I sensed his sadness. Somehow, I cannot play this act. The words are optimistic and the face smiles but the heart is so heavy. I feel everyone is awaiting my 'rebirth', but I cannot deliver this 'package'.

I had a word with God today about why His plan included all this pain, from which there is no relief. I know I must trust more in the inevitable resolution of all the contradictions, instead of trying to make sense of it all.

Martin has returned from University to share a place under these heavy clouds with us. You are the focal point, Stephen. Your life gave us laughter and optimism, and your death strengthened our love and longing for something higher than this place. We want you to share with us a special kind of silence. You can never really leave us. I think you know that.

There are even more cards this Christmas, with consoling messages and prayers for all of us. It is comforting to find that other people want to help us with our sad journey for a while. I knew I would be unable to 'make the grade' this Christmas, if I stayed at home; so many memories. So I arranged for Mark, Martin and Andrew with your father and I to spend the few days of the holiday away on the Continent. We left the 'worker' (Paul) and the 'student' (Brian) at home, with plenty of supplies.

None of us felt like celebrating, so it was better we were away in a strange place. We had a pleasant lunch, without the usual razzamatazz. It seemed strange to go into a foreign church on Christmas Day. One nice surprise was that the Mass was sung in Latin; I actually remembered all the words, although it must be twenty years since I sang those words.

Christmas Eve was marred a little by an 'event' taking place. Well, we couldn't take Mark with us without something happening, could we? He went with Martin to have a quiet drink in one of the taverns and they got into the company of some Italians. He managed to get their backs up by asking them which side they were on during the war, as they seemed to change sides so often! This remark resulted in a physical attack by the Italians on Martin, who was just drinking his beer in quiet contentment. He did a 'Ghandi' and refused to retaliate. Your dear brother Mark joined in the war, minus his glasses (yes, he wears glasses now), so his vision was impaired. Christmas Day was greeted with one black eye from each of them and an afternoon rest!

On Boxing Day, young Andrew helped himself to a glass of vodka and was violently sick. As this episode happened just prior to the evening meal, your father and I did a shuttle-run to and from the dining table to assist the helpless form

31

in the bedroom. Apart from these few hiccups, it was a reasonable break! I can hear you laughing, Stephen!

We visited your grave before the holiday and covered it with flowers and Christmas plants. Your father and I stood there for quite some time, talking about you and wondering where you were. We looked really lost souls, standing there together, wishing you a Happy Christmas. I hope you heard us, Stephen, and realised how much you meant to us both. You see, you were never a parent yourself, Stephen, so you could not realise what it is like to bring a child into the world and to love him and see him grow into a young man, only to have him blow out, like a candle flame. You wonder what it was all about, but no one gives you any real answers.

January

We have now reached January. I am not feeling very well this month. My mind keeps going back to 'that night'. There is an aura around; a strange kind of tension, like a bomb about to go off. I wish I was anywhere but here. God seems far away and you seem far away too.

Everyone expects me to get back to what I used to be. They seem to be waiting. Don't they know that I will never be that person again? I realise now more than ever how much everyone hates change. It disrupts and therefore it frightens people. They want things to remain as they were and that cannot be. Each experience in life alters us and we change, and that must happen if we are to move on to the next phase in our lives. The deeper the experience, the deeper is the change.

32

I looked at your photographs tonight, all of them, and the last one you had taken — in the kitchen — was especially poignant. You had let your hair grow long on top and I remember saying to you, about a week before you died, "You *must* get your hair cut." "What's the matter with it?" you answered, "I've just washed it."

I could not help thinking of the note you left when you died. You said you could not see anything in mind or body of which you could be particularly proud. I will never again make a comment about anyone's appearance, unless it is a complimentary one. I feel at this moment that I am an ogre and that it is all my fault. The lessons I am learning about myself are the hardest lessons I have ever had to learn. I turned back the pages of the photograph album, to your school photograph, the one — you will remember it — where you said you looked like Dr Spock. You looked so quiet and happy. All your pictures showed that contented smile, though I must admit that there was also a rather strange air of vulnerability about you — or am I reading more into that face of yours than I used to see?

I dreamt about you last night, Stephen, for the first time since the day after you died. In the dream, I was asleep in bed and you were lying on the floor beside me. You had a young child, lying next to you, but I could not recognise him. You were wearing Andrew's sweater. I called your name, but my voice was slurred, as though I could not speak properly. You turned around and looked at me, but I felt you did not know me. Strangely, I did not get upset about this. You looked much younger, about twelve years old. When I awakened, I wondered if it was possible that you were growing up again, in another dimension. If you are, I hope that one day you will tell me all about it.

I have had odd new feelings throughout this month of January, almost as though I am going through the whole thing again, in a different way. Somehow, you seem closer to me now and I can catch the feeling of you at a much deeper level. My only difficulty is getting rid of the human attachment — re-living your last days and what I could have done for you. These thoughts do not come as often now, but when they do it's like a force inside of me, trying to get out. Even when I am not concentrating on you, I will suddenly cry out with a raging wail. It is as though I have to get rid of something physically. On other days, I can think of you and smile, even laugh, recalling our happy conservations and that whacky grin of yours. No one can ever take that away from me. The happy years we spent together are ours and even God does not take them away. They happened to us and what has been, has been and will remain.

It is the little things that lift me high above the clouds. Do you remember the time you were playfully mocking me and I said "I'll box your ears"? I did a mock interpretation of a boxer, dancing like Mohammed Ali and tapping your ears. You collapsed, laughing. Then there are the little things that take me down into the depths, like the time you and Andrew were fighting and I screamed at you and said you should know better. You went away and returned with wet eyes. My anger may or may not have been justified, but oh, how those eyes haunt me now!

I must be making some progress because I am beginning to think about the rest of the family. I see Paul's face after he found you. I thought he was having a heart attack but when I looked into his eyes, I knew he wanted to tell me something and could not. I remember saying the word 'death'. "It's death, isn't it?" I screamed. "Yes, yes, I think it is," he said, and then looking at me despairingly he said "Yes, it is." Now he says "There is such a vast emptiness that somehow cannot be filled." He concentrates on his own relationship with you, Stephen. It is something only he knows about and it helps him. "So long as we don't try to understand from a human level, we will become closer and closer to him," he says. I still feel that he has problems with the emptiness.

We talk about the year before when there were only the four of us at home and there are times when he feels that if one of your other brothers had been there, instead of him, you would not have taken your life. He has had to come to terms with the feeling that he was inadequate to help you. It could have happened after you started University in some lonely room, miles away from home. If that was the other alternative, then he can accept all the pain and suffering that put him in the position of finding your dead body. He doesn't think he could have stood hearing that you had died this way, in some distant place.

Your father struggles on in his own inimitable way but he finds great difficulty in getting rid of those first few moments, when he tried to bring you round, knowing there was no hope. He was completely shattered by the experience. You know that he always had a very soft spot for you and is now so glad that he stood up one day last summer, in your presence, and admitted that you had never caused him one ounce of pain. He still feels that you did so much for him, and that he did not do half enough for you. He keeps his sorrow to himself most times, but that does not prevent him from weeping unashamedly when he hears music or visits your grave.

You told us that you knew there would be a gap when you had gone, a gap even bigger because we are a large family, but I don't think you ever realised how much you personally would be missed. It's strange how much we take for granted, until we do not have it any more; even stranger that other people do not see such a tragedy ever happening to them. We did not. It is the kind of thing that happens to other people, not us.

I have been told many times how you must have been con-
templating this act for quite a while, but now I know, more
than I know anything, that this was not so. The line between
carrying on with life and giving it up is a very fine one, and
we are all capable of crossing it, given particular circumstances. I consider myself too egotistical to give up on life,
but lately I have been so wrapped up in my own despairing
feelings and so very close to that line, that I now realise that
rationality can disappear when you feel so low. Other people
do not enter into your mind because everything is narrowed
down to this blackness.

Suicide is an act, not the contemplation of an act. For
you, a plastic bag just happened to be there. We cannot get
rid of everything that is a potential danger to us, although I
will never again see a plastic bag as a handy little carrier. I
have to admit that as soon as I empty the shopping, I throw
the bag away; even touching the surface of one gives me a
physical feeling of repulsion. You see, Stephen, you were
nine months being formed inside of me, and hours being
born and years being cared for and loved — and a plastic
bag had the final say.

These days I pray often for you and us, and I remember a
hexagram in the *I Ching*. It refers to release and talks about
'the deep below' and the 'thunder above'. There is an example
from the condemned soldier's tale in *The Idiot*. On his ride
to the gallows, instead of concentrating on his danger and
almost hopeless chances of salvation, the condemned man
gives up his ego and slips into a vision of a religious nature.
In the final five minutes, he enters a new dimension, as though
he were seeing his surroundings for the first time. At the
very last minute, he gains a reprieve and is saved. In vain he
struggles to capture that last-minute vision again and ends
up dying, five years later, of alcoholism.

My danger is that I know one day I will be released from
this acute emotional pain and so I must not go on a high
note about this release. There will be a great spiritual loss,

36

as I have leaned heavily on God recently. A very low time will accompany my re-entry into the normal world. It will be necessary, for your sake and mine, to gain something from this terrible experience, so that your life and your death have meaning for all of us.

As a start to this eventual release, I realise I have to purge myself once and for all. This will mean sinking to the very bottom before I can rise again. In an attempt at this purging ceremony, I looked into my almost-empty diary for 1985 and came across only three entries which read as follows:

Wednesday 10th July, 1985
I have strong feelings today. No matter how much I try to hide from it, something is wrong. I feel I am waiting for something to happen, but I don't know what it is. All of this year I have been aware of an anxious feeling, but today it is very strong.

Monday 12th August, 1985
Stephen took his life today, in the early hours of this morning. He left a long note, absolving us from any blame. He said he knew how much we loved him but he could not manage to love himself. He put a plastic bag over his head, lay in the pantry and died. My life is over; I am desolate; no pain is as great as this. It is the ultimate pain of my life.

Friday 16th August, 1985
I went to see Stephen's body today. He looked so young and beautiful, but he was not there. He was cold and hard except for his hair, which was soft and warm. He knew I would love to touch his hair. Oh, my lovely Stephen. Why is your body lying here? They say that for the branches of a tree to reach into heaven, its roots must have reached into hell.

Two bright sunny days have given way to another dark miserable Monday. How I hate those mud-coloured skies! Do you remember that March day in 1984, when you and I and Andrew boarded the plane for Dhahran? We were very excited. We were going to spend a month in Saudi Arabia with your father. Having never really seen much of the world, we could not believe that we were now going to enjoy the trip of a lifetime. I was the only one worried about the flight. You and Andrew sat there as though you were quite used to jetting around.

British Airways certainly excelled themselves foodwise. You commented on the lovely tender steak and crisp vegetables. When the plane began to rock, due to turbulence over the desert, I need not have worried about you two — you were both fast asleep!

Stepping off the plane into that beautiful warm evening air, I had the strange feeling I had visited this place before. There was an odd smell of oldness about it. I remember you making a joke about it, saying my sense of smell was so keen, I could smell a match being struck three streets away! We had a lovely relaxing time. You even started to play football again and actually sun-bathed by the pool. I remember you laughing most of the time and thoroughly enjoying the company of your father's friends. You never looked as well as you did there. You must have been made for the sun, Stephen, for it mellowed the serious side of your personality. I am so very happy we had that time together.

This last week of January is proving to be very difficult. I have become 'semi-detached' as it were, and feel that I am watching myself doing things. When I speak it is as though I am programmed to do so. They are not my own words.

A gloom has descended upon the house; Brian is suffering from a leg injury and the remainder of the family is in a state of weird depression. All of them seem to lose their tempers and this controlled voice of mine rings out to redress the balance. I wonder how much longer I can keep up this faked normality?

38

The American Shuttle blew up, and seven people died. I watched it on television, dry-eyed. Listening to President Reagan's monologue about America, I realise that the man is married to that land. He sees nothing but his personal dream. Why doesn't he sit down and ponder on the possibility that the accident was a warning and his 'Star Wars' dream way 'off target'? I suspect he believes he will live on to make an American Universe and become the complete controller of the heavens. What a foolish man!

They are even bringing in psychologists to help the young people who suffered the effects of the death of their teacher in the shuttle. Thousands died last year from starvation, volcanoes and other terrible disasters. Some lost their whole families. I cannot remember such personal care being offered to them. My loss seems small in comparison to these major events but I am still finding it almost impossible to bear. Unless I, physically and mentally, fall apart, there will certainly be no psychological help offered to me or my family. It was suggested that if I needed to relax, I should take a swim each morning. I wonder if the person who suggested that knows that the fact that I actually get out of bed to face each day is a miracle in itself? I think not.

The effort needed to face the strain grows daily. I realise everyone has problems but I need distance now between myself and others. I do not even want to talk about your death with anyone else. To escape for a while and find quiet contentment would perhaps help the healing process. Amongst crowds, I feel isolated; alone I feel some kind of peace. It is probably because I have not been allowed just to be.

I am much quieter lately because I am living somewhere in my own head. I keep coming face to face with lines from your final letter. Today I remember the line — "could not manage to achieve the ultimate necessity of loving myself". Obviously, Stephen, when you looked at the world as a young, intelligent person, you were aware that most people manage to love themselves without very much effort. It is true to say that we, as a family, are highly critical of ourselves — I don't know the reason for that. When I feel better, I intend to adopt and preach a new philosophy. Any job or goal or task will be tackled from the premise "I am as good as or better than the people already out there". There is a need to give myself and others who need confidence this ego-boost if we are ever to take the first step.

There is so much confusion in my mind at the moment. Perhaps I have tried to get back to normality too fast and my body is giving me a warning. Physically I ache all over and have actually vomited many times. In between bouts of nausea, I have cried desperately and an overwhelming sadness has enveloped me. I am not concentrating on sadness; it is just that I seem unable to make the necessary effort to pull out of it.

Your father has helped me all he can and feels that I need a time to rest. This would seem sensible except that rest makes me feel worse. The weather is certainly very, very bad, indescribably cold with easterly winds.

How I hate that wind! We used to talk about the wind, didn't we, Stephen, as though it were a person, because it made us so irritable and anxious. I read a scientific book recently, about the effects of the wind on our metabolism. It appears we were not alone, Stephen. Our feelings are shared by much greater minds than ours.

I have accepted that you are gone and will not come back, but there is an immense difference between that and the fact that you are not here and I will not see you again in this life. You have gone — that is a fact — but living with you not here is so much harder.

It suddenly hit me today, as I was surrounded by boys from your old school, on the bus coming home. My eyes always search out your old school tie, then I turn away and listen to their voices. Today they were discussing a biology experiment and talking about some field trip. For a moment I imagined you were at the University. Then I began to think nostalgically of the field trip you went on in 1984, recalling the amusing incident of the soup. You told us all about the 'disgusting' soup, which was so bad that everyone left it; everyone that is except the teacher who accompanied you. He commented on how good it was and proceeded to eat three bowls full! He could never understand what you all found so amusing. Suddenly I was gazing through the window of the bus with tears streaming down my face. You are not at University, Stephen, you are not here at all; that is why I am crying.

I wish the lady in the bank would not be so pleasant. She knows about you taking your life. I blurted it out one day to her friend, who must have told her. I used to do that. I had this compulsion to tell everyone I met about you. It somehow made you seem alive. Now she looks at me with that face and I become confused, almost apologetic. I am afraid of suddenly saying "Yes, I'm the lady whose son killed himself. Please do not treat me differently, because you make me feel guilty and he would not like that. He never meant to hurt me. It was just something he did without thinking. If he had been killed in a car crash you would not look at me like that."

The sun is shining today, although it still continues to snow and that cold easterly wind blows incessantly. I read a story in a magazine about some woman dying. The actual death took up only three lines of the story, as the main theme was her life. In fact, her death was a complete non-event, almost as though it were irrelevant. There was a happy ending and the remaining characters went on to live full and happy lives. For some reason, I started to cry and took out the album I had made up of all your photographs. This upset me even more. I noticed that in all the pictures of you and I together, we were always laughing. I know you would hate to see me the way I look now, but please tell me why you left, Stephen, without saying goodbye? I need to know why someone so full of life and humour decided to finish off that life. Do you realise how much we need you? Oh yes, we are all together, but in our sorrow each one of us is isolated within ourselves. Occasionally I get glimpses of what someone else is feeling. Paul mentioned the strain of living through you. Everything he does is done in your name. He cannot help it. He knows it is wrong and it is wearing him out, but he feels guilty like the rest of us.

You said in your letter that no one was to blame, absolutely no one else. It was all *your* fault, and you did not want us to feel guilty. You were so young, Stephen, that you did not realise that we would all blame ourselves; mountains and mountains of guilt building up inside each and everyone of us, which will surely take a lifetime to remove.

During your inquest, the people in the court were looking at us for some kind of explanation. I cannot think why there was an inquest. I told them you were not involved with drugs. Of course they did not believe me, so they had to cut you up to find out. There was nothing wrong with you, they said, so why did you take your own life? They even came to the conclusion that your note was not a good enough reason, and that the balance of your mind must have been disturbed. After all, why would you kill yourself for no other reason than that you saw nothing in yourself worth offering to the world, or because you felt you would not fit in at University? Unfortunately, Stephen, people want an explanation that fits into their understanding. Over-dosing on drugs would have been acceptable by the 'powers-that-be' because drugs are an accepted modern menace. Even the doctor told me on that terrible morning that there was a chance you could have been saved if you had decided to commit suicide with drugs. If you had experienced girl-friend trouble or been a homo-sexual or an un-wanted child or found that your parents were seeking a divorce, then this would have made their records nice and neat. They could not cope with a bright intelligent boy from a loving family with a brilliant University career ahead of him putting a plastic bag over his head and saying "I can see no other alternative". This just 'rocks the system', Stephen.

I realise that you did not create the system and perhaps young people today need something different; some way in which they can feel useful and needed instead of being forced to concentrate on their own needs and aspirations. I cannot change the system, I can change only myself, and your death has certainly brought about a change in me. I know there is a long, long way to go, but slowly I am beginning to lose my sense of fear.

As the days go by, I am beginning to feel a different person and realising that physical death is not the end of it all. I expect others will think that I am just looking for some kind of comfort; only *I* know this is not so. You are still around, Stephen, even if it is in some other dimension that I do not understand. Love is a very strange but strong quality. When a person physically dies, the love does not die but remains within the people who are left. There must be some reason for this. In spite of my shaky belief in the afterworld, I know I will see you again one day. I don't know when or why or how, but this feeling goes beyond believing or desiring; a kind of certain knowledge that this will happen.

Thank goodness we have reached the end of February with its snow and wind and rain. How is it that this shortest month of the year has always seemed the longest to me and never more than this year?

March

I haven't been down to your grave for a few weeks. The weather has been very bad but that was not the reason. Somehow I have purposely avoided going there. I even made excuses not to go. In my head, I keep hearing you say that you are not there and that I can communicate with you anytime, anywhere. I know that, Stephen. In fact, sometimes when I get upset (usually when I am on my own), I apologise to you. I say "I'm sorry, Stephen, I don't mean to act this way." Then I hear you tell me that you are fine and that there is no need to worry about you. I suppose, being merely human, I need some tangible evidence and I am certainly not getting it when I visit your grave.

Talking to Andrew the other day made me realise how young children can be so accurate in their simplicity. He said "It would not be so bad, Mum, if we could write him a letter and know that he received it, but they don't have letters in heaven, do they?" Physical death has such a cutting edge. It severs human links for ever. Surely there is more to life than death? If only we were capable of rolling the past, present and future into one whole, getting rid of the 'then', 'now' and 'tomorrow'.

Some forms of Buddhism advocate that only 'now' is important and that we must not hope, anticipate or worry about what has been or might be. I feel the need to merge all forms of being into one, so that I am not bogged down with sad memories or future hopes. What I need will, of

44

course, not happen. There will be no magic wand waved — only times that have to be got through, no matter how long it takes.

I am beginning to ask myself about the changes I have made since you left, Stephen.

The first thing I did was to go back to the faith I once so strongly followed. I needed some answers from God, so I prayed for them. He has helped me considerably, although of course He will never tell me the whole story. From the time I was a small child, I have always prayed to God, never Christ or one of the saints. I always figured that if anyone knew the answer, God would. If He was responsible for the creation of the Universe, what would be the use of asking anyone else? The road would be much longer any other way.

Recently, I have communicated a great deal with God and I have realised, with amazing clarity, that if you had not died I would not have given my spiritual life very much thought until I was too old to do anything about it. I would of course have prayed occasionally, but I would not have given to it the importance I give to it now. Does that mean that you had to die for me to realise how necessary my spiritual life was? How terrible! I feel so pathetic, especially knowing that you took the spiritual side of your nature very seriously.

Once again, I feel I have let you down. If I had carried on bringing you up with the religious practices I taught you from the beginning, you might have found some solace there, in your hour of real need. It would also have given you extra strength to know you had the backing of your family. For many years you read the New Testament every day and only stopped this practice a few months before you died.

Praying alone is certainly difficult in our present society; even praying at all is considered to be odd. The very mention of God or anything religious causes panic among many of our modern friends. How could I ever let you be so lonely? Why didn't I join you? Well, it is my turn to pray alone now, Stephen, and ask the God you always believed in to listen.

I have also made another change. Instead of just handing over donations to the Third World, I have sponsored a child in Africa which means that I will become directly involved by writing to him or her and forming a personal link. This way, the problems of the starving children out there become more real and not just a picture on a television screen, which I can shut out by the turn of a knob. It also brings home to your brothers just how desperate the situation is out there when they realise that the princely sum of just over £7 per month is the difference between a child living or dying. If this is all it costs then one child dying of hunger is one too many. Your death has certainly made us stop in our tracks, look at our lives and start to move in a completely different direction.

Martin, your closest brother, is 21 today and we sent him all the greetings and good wishes that go with that milestone. Knowing him, I feel he will experience much sadness because of your absence. It's funny how birthdays bring everything back. They are markers along the way, and make you think of those closest to you and what they mean to your life.

Today was definitely a 'Stephen day'; the kind of day when the temperature suddenly changed and a warm breeze blew. It was a day of promise somehow, with just a hint of the winter sun. I half expected you to come through the door and make some witty comment about Martin being 'an old man' now.

The following morning brought bright blue skies and brilliant sunshine — surely the first day of spring. The promise of yesterday had been fulfilled — except that you were not there to share it. It's strange how I miss you even more when the sun shines; maybe because it does not shine in quite the same way for me any more. Positively, I decided to set about washing curtains and covers and I opened all the windows wide.

I must admit I need your presence badly and find it impossible to believe you are not coming today. My resolutions are quite strong but my will is amazingly weak. Perhaps it's because we are in the period of Lent — forty days in the desert and all that; I certainly feel very much alone. I will try to accept this time without complaint and look forward to Easter and, hopefully, a new beginning.

My mind wandered back to your eighteenth birthday, the year before you died. I remember buying you a radio cassette player and some expensive jeans. It did occur to me at the time that I should have completed the gift, with the addition of a decent pair of earphones. All I see now is you going into the front room to listen to some music. If you had been given the earphones, you could have sat with the rest of us and not felt so lonely and maybe, even, you would still be here with us. Silly I know; forgive me, I'm just clutching at straws. In retrospect, there appear to be so many things I did wrong.

I am not indulging in self-pity, just looking for reasons and, if I am absolutely honest, I am not yet really finding one good enough to explain your absence. The week after you died, I told your best friend that if you could appear to us now, you would probably put your head round the door and, with a weak grin, say "Sorry fellas, I went a bit over the top there." He agreed and said "That's exactly what he would do."

We all really know that you made a rash decision, and then went through with it. The pain comes for all of us in living with the enormity of your decision. It was the final decision, between life and death, and you were not given a chance to change it. Because we were not given the chance of discussing it with you, we will probably spend years trying to find out how you came to that point. Deep down we are really thinking about ourselves and the pain we are experiencing in missing you.

I have just spent two days in bed with influenza. I cannot remember how long it is since I was ill enough to stay in bed. My mind wandered as my temperature rose and I seemed to be suffering from strange hallucinations. I could not remember whether you had actually died or I was just imagining it. When I felt a little better, physically, I realised the truth. I started to cry and could not stop; gentle, continual crying. There must still be so much pain inside. Will I ever get rid of it all?

Still feeling weak, I got up and moved back into the normal routine. In many ways I liken the pain of your death to the pain of your birth; harsh and unremitting, with no room for anything else. That is the only similarity, for with your birth the pain was forgotten in the joy of a new life and its hopes and dreams. With your death, there is nothing, and I am left with a continual dull ache, which greets me every morning and remains with me until I am lost in sleep each night. The harshness has gone but the ache is not unlike the continual pain following major surgery, which can last for some considerable time.

It is the effort involved in appearing normal that is so wearing. There was a time, a few months ago, when tears would relieve the ache a little; not any more. Tears are just a part of each day now, as I struggle alone to come to terms with your non-existence. Everyone seems to have abandoned me — you, God, everyone. This is the point of no return. I will either sink even lower or I will survive. I need help but I am not sure where to look for it.

In desperation I called up a leading astrologer, telling him that the counsellor needed a counsellor. He was very kind and felt that I needed some kind of psychological guidance, because I was allowing my own spiritual needs to go begging. He suggested that I get in touch with a lady who practised psychosynthesis, which deals with the spiritual side of our natures. I had never heard of it before but I was willing to try anything.

I went along to meet the lady in question and spent an hour and a half discussing how this method of help could possibly assist me. I half-expected some deep psychological method, such as hypnosis, on which I was not really keen. However, I was pleasantly surprised. It appears that the founder of psychosynthesis was a man called Roberto Assagiolo who, half a century ago, was developing this method. Until the last decade, his work has not been very well-known, but it is now gaining considerable ground. It is an extension of psychoanalysis in the sense that it goes beyond the depth psychology of latent biological drives and urges that Freud emphasised, to include a 'height psychology' dealing with what is 'right' about us; that is, what is good, beautiful, compassionate, purposeful and so on, but does not have a chance to express itself because we are not allowing it to come through.

The aim of psychosynthesis is not to change us but to give us support in removing the blocks arresting our development. It advocates that no matter how distressed someone is, with time and the appropriate support they will find what they are looking for. It is likened to climbing a mountain, your mountain, with someone who knows more about climbing mountains than you do. In no way are they going to climb the mountain for you or carry you up there, because it is your mountain and only you have the real answer to your own life.

Unfortunately, people — English people especially — take the attitude that if you are involved in psychology in any way it means you are sick. I know I am not sick, just somewhat off balance at the moment because of this particular crisis in my life. It has made me lop-sided in the sense that your death has become the focal point of my life, to the exclusion of all else, even my own basic psychological needs. They certainly need nurturing.

Do you remember how, when Paul finished University and was trying to get a job, he used to spend hours solving mathematical puzzles? He would leave reams of paper all over the place. Every room you went into, there was sure to be a paper with a maths equation on it. We would all laugh and say that he would end up plastering the walls with mathematical formulæ. It was as though he was afraid of forgetting all he had learned. As soon as he got a job, the practice ceased. Well, now he has a new obsession, Stephen. Ever since he found your body, he writes poetry, pages and pages of it. It is a desperate kind of poetry, moving between despair and anger. He seems to be searching for some kind of escape, but I am sure that, in his soul, he knows there is none. I pray for him so often, that the image of what he found that day will eventually blur in his mind, so that he will not be able to recall the exact picture.

You never thought about the aftermath, Stephen, did you? I know you didn't. You saw only the future, so bleak for you and you thought we would all get over it and accept that it was a decision you had to make. I have to tell you that it will take us years to accept that it has happened at all, and it will leave scars that will never really heal. We keep apologising for feeling this way because we put no blame whatsoever upon you. We really wish we could say that we accept your decision was right, but we cannot.

Every act a person commits affect others in some way, like the ripple from a pebble tossed into a pool. The effects move outwards and continue to spread. So, although we cannot accept your decision, something has definitely happened to us. We were always a close family, in the sense that we cared about and communicated with each other, but now an invisible bond has been strengthened and our tongues are loosened. We talk freely about God, our spiritual beliefs and what they mean or do not mean to us. There is no embarrassment because we have nothing to hide now. There is real freedom when there is nothing left to lose and what do we have to lose now, except our own lives?

When you died, it felt as if the whole world died that day. If all of the people I know and love had died that morning, I could not have felt any more desolation. I was wrong. We cannot be alone if we identify so much with other human beings. Our humanity then serves a purpose and makes us aware of the gift God gave to us — Love.

St Patrick's Day dawned and took me back to my youth, when my father used to receive a large box of wet shamrock from his native Ireland. It would be divided equally between us and we would tie our bunch with green ribbon and wear it proudly all day. The evening would be celebrated with Irish songs and dancing and it was the only day in the year when my father drank too much. I could always tell because, usually, he was a very serious man. On St Patrick's Day however, he never stopped laughing. I can still remember the words and music of the Irish songs and they never fail to move me.

On this particular Irish feast day, your father and I listened to an Irish concert. We sat in separate chairs for over an hour with tears just rolling down. My own tears were no surprise but I had never seen your father cry for that length of time. When it was over, he came across to me and, kneeling down, he just held on to me, completely oblivious of his sons sitting around. There were no apologies when he recovered, just a statement that Irish music and some particular hymns stirred up something in his soul and took away any control he thought he might have had.

You were right, your father did think highly of you and he is finding it very difficult. I know what he means about the Irish ballads. Maybe it's an echo from our roots, reminding us of what we once were. Whatever it is, it cannot be ignored when it erupts like a volcano, weeping its hot way through our bodies. It makes your absence even more painful, almost as though a physical part of me has left for some other dimension. The physical and emotional become one, as I am made aware of the fact that you were once inside me. Our lives were joined as one and now that you are not here, there is a physical feeling that I am not completely whole, that a part of my anatomy has died.

I am slowly becoming totally detached. Although I am living, breathing and working, my responses are robotic and uninvolved. Perhaps there is too much information coming in at me and I have switched on to 'hold'. Your father has just taken up a new position with a computer firm and on the day he started he was offered another position in the Middle East, which would mean Andrew and I going out there to live, later in the year. I was asked what I thought about it but could give no real response because I just don't feel anything about it. I am simply here, a functioning machine, or 'keeping still' as the *I Ching* would say. I feel it's my *Tao* to 'keep still' at the moment.

I had a thought the other day — "It's such a long time since I've seen you, Stephen." What is the matter with me? Am I holding on because I expect I will be seeing you, that you will be coming home? I know full well that you are not going to come home so why do I think it's a long time? I must realise that I cannot 'get back to normal' because getting back to the normality I knew would be having you around. I have to create a new normality, without you.

Easter will soon be upon us. I have not looked forward to Easter for many years. In fact I have hated it, probably because of my early childhood days. I remember the sadness when I went to church on Maundy Thursday and did my 'hourly watch'. I used to think of this Christ-person, sitting in the Garden of Gethsemane, alone with no one to share the pain, and then Good Friday, when they nailed Him to the cross. I was so worn out by sadness that I missed the Resurrection. I could never understand all that purple and darkness through Holy Week and then suddenly on Easter Sunday, flowers, brightness and white vestments. Did everyone forget so easily?

It is different now. I feel I have been through the forty days in the desert, personally, with no one to share the pain and I have been carrying a heavy cross these last eight months. Dear God, I hope I don't miss the Resurrection this year.

Your brothers keep playing the music you used to listen to, and somehow I cannot take it yet. Your father asks "Who is this?" of a tape you played constantly. Mark mentions certain lines he really loves. Are they so insensitive? Where were they when you were playing this music? Oh yes, I remember now. Your father was out in Saudi Arabia and Mark was in Africa. Why are mothers there all the time, so that they can recall every painful minute? Everyone else appears to remember fragments and scenes from your life, while I seem to have been given a front row seat for the whole play.

I suppose it could be said that I am experiencing withdrawal symptoms. I am having to get used to living without you. Even if I recover, I will always be a mother who bore a son and lost him at the age of eighteen years and eight months, when he took his own life. Nothing will ever change that. I do not want to believe that is true, because it is far too horrific. For the very first time I screamed at God "Why did You take my son? Why didn't You help him when he needed You? He never did anyone any harm, including You. I really hate Your plan." I didn't feel any better afterwards, but had to admit to myself that I was so wrapped up in my own self-pity that it would have been impossible to have gained any understanding at this time.

I should be letting go of my attachment to you now, but something is keeping me hanging on. At first I thought it was guilt, maybe it was in a way. In retrospect, I think about all those things I could have done. That isn't the real reason however. I do not want to let go because I do not want you to be forgotten. When I think about that, how stupid can I be? How could you ever be forgotten? It would be like saying that I could forget my own existence.

I am really a very lucky person — all those sons who care what happens to me and your father willing me to recover. All those years when you were here, Stephen, and the fun we had. You said you wanted to be remembered for all the laughs we shared together. There must have been some bad times, but I cannot recall them. It is very strange, but I miss you most when I hear an amusing story I know you would like. I was talking to Andrew about this and he said "Oh he can hear you all right — he's not missing anything." His absolute confidence in heaven stuns me sometimes. He says it with such authority.

My mother entered my thoughts the other day, probably because it was her birthday this month. She was a lady of simple faith — no delving into theology for her. As far as she was concerned, God was up there listening to her prayers and if things did not turn out right, then that was how it was meant to be. When she was sad, she cried; when she was happy, she laughed. If she disagreed with anyone, she would say so and there would be no explanations for that either! Her opinion was that explanations were completely unnecessary and wasted a large amount of energy, which could be put to better use.

I was the youngest of the family so there were great expecta-
tions of me. I felt I had too many guides, in the form of
brothers, a sister and many aunts. Everyone knew what was
best for me. You were the youngest for seven years, Stephen
— did *you* feel that way? It is such a responsibility to be the
youngest. Others think you are having an easy ride, being
guided and cossetted, when all you really want is to lead
your own life and make your own decisions. There is all this
guilt about appearing ungrateful; as you know everyone is
doing it because they love you. It can be difficult to find
your own identity with all that help around.

At the moment, I am preparing a script for a conference I
have been asked to attend. The conference is about a student's
first year at University and it was felt that because I had
personal experience of this, having had five sons go through
the system, I could describe real case histories. I obviously
feel very strongly about it, especially since you said that your
trouble began when you visited the University and realised
you would not fit in. Your brothers' experiences of their first
years were not exactly wonderful, and I am now beginning
to wonder if listening to their stories had also put you off?
So much information coming in at from all sides about the
problems and the loneliness; worry about the examinations
and whether or not decent accommodation could be found;
the amount of work to be done and how the money always
seemed to run out. You must have felt completely awash
with it.

And then there was that terrible barren time between the
end of 'A' level examinations and your entry into University
in October. No wonder you did not make it. The television
and newspapers were full of disasters — air crashes, hi-jacks,
a massive earthquake, the eruption of a volcano. There were
thousands dead, and many families grieving. And if that wasn't
enough, the media decided to give us days of coverage on
the fortieth anniversary of the Hiroshima bombing.

The sun hardly shone at all that summer and you were left with acres of time on your hands. I remember you were very tired after your examinations but I did not really worry about that, because your brothers had been exactly the same. I also remember trying to get you off on a walking holiday with Martin, but you said, in a jocular way, that you really did not have the energy. You must have been trying to see where you fitted into this world and, with all that information blasting in at you, you could not quite find the place. Now I say, if only you had hung on a little longer, if only . . ., if only . . .

Someone sent me a verse written by Gerard Manley-Hopkins called *Heaven-Haven*. It's actually about a nun taking the veil, but it so fits you at this time of utter confusion.

> *I have desired to go*
> *Where springs not fail*
> *To fields where flies no sharp and sided hail*
> *And a few lilies grow.*
>
> *And I have asked to be*
> *Where no storms come*
> *Where the green swell is in the havens dumb*
> *And out of the swing of the sea.*

I do hope Stephen, with all my being, that your desire was fulfilled.

I did not miss the Resurrection this Easter, although there were times of doubt. There was no bargain with God. I just decided to attend the Easter services from Maundy Thursday through to Easter Sunday with a belief that I would learn something valuable from the experience and rid myself of childhood memories. The church on Maundy Thursday evening was optimistic as usual, full of flowers and candles and there was something gently rewarding in seeing the priest wash the feet of ordinary parishioners. I went alone because your father could not get home in time from work.

Your father came with me on Good Friday afternoon to face the absolute starkness of that day. The giant wooden cross above the altar had been removed, to be carried down the centre of the church by the Deacon. He kept pausing along the way while we sang "This is the wood of the cross, on which hung the Saviour of the world". I thought of you and of the many others who carry crosses and how no man can carry another man's cross. I felt a great sadness, and could not sing some of the hymns because I put you in the place of Christ — "He did no wrong, He put His trust in God". I thought of how I had always felt completely in control of situations and that I did not particularly need anything higher than my own intelligence. And then, when you died, how I rushed back to beg for help from God, to whom I hadn't spoken for a long time. Were the words right? Did you "suffer so that we could walk, on the very road that you trod, like sheep who had gone astray, till you led us back to God"?

I was completely exhausted by the end of the service, but I had to carry out my intention of seeing through the Easter ceremonies. Unfortunately, the priest went on and on about the wonderful Resurrection and, instead of just living for the moment, he planted expectation in my mind. Up to this point, I had not hoped or expected anything, I had just experienced the time I was in. So, when it came to the vigil on Easter Saturday and the candles, and the flowers, and the singing, I felt nothing at all.

On the Monday something quite strange happened. We had a family celebration at my brother's house and at one point, I was subtly insulted by a member of the family. I was surprised to find myself laughing and feeling no animosity or anger. It did not really matter to me and I began to realise just what the Resurrection meant. It was not in church that I would find it, it was only by going out into the world and facing my particular cross in a new way. Those days of meditation and sadness had meant something to me. I had to face the world in which I live and, in spite of my heavier cross, learn to laugh at myself and others and the petty opinions we all feel are so important.

My three-year-old great-nephew was there enjoying the fact that he could now speak sentences. He was telling himself jokes and falling off the seat laughing. Oh what a joy to see such innocence! I felt I was on his wavelength, at least for one day.

April

Your father took the job in Abu Dhabi and we had four days to pack all his equipment and see him off. It was so disorientating, I can hardly believe it has happened. I will miss him tremendously, as his presence gave me the strength to relax a little over these past months. I know he will miss us as he will be alone out there with no one to share his loss.

Why do I feel that cool wind again around my face, Stephen? Are you trying to tell me something? Or perhaps your father is trying to let me know that, like you, he is always really with us. I wonder if we will eventually end up in Abu Dhabi, as planned, later in the year? No, I must not start wondering, hoping, expecting. I must just get on with today.

It is strange how we become so attached to some people and then, when they are physically present, we feel we have lost them. I am beginning to learn that it is not so. It is the person to whom we become attached, the essential being, the something that makes them unique, so why do we associate that with the necessary presence of a physical body? We all have imagination and feelings and that person can be just as real to us in the absence of their physical presence —

sometimes even more so — because there are no physical distractions.

I am slowly realising that when someone close to us dies, or is absent even for a while, they never really go. They had existed for us in this world and so they will continue to do so. All we need to do is think about them and gradually the spirit of that person is with us in all its uniqueness. We do not just experience a picture of a physical body in our minds, we see movement, laughter, tears, conversation and the essential essence of that person and the love that was shared. We even feel that person within us. You are as special as you always were, Stephen, simply because you existed.

I received a card, some time ago, from a priest I have never even met. There was a prayer on the card which said

> *"We seem to give them back to you,*
> *you who gave them to us.*
> *Yet you did not lose them by giving them to us,*
> *So we do not lose them by their return to you.*
> *What you give to us, you never really take away.*
> *Life is eternal and love is immortal*
> *and death is only an horizon*
> *And an horizon is nothing but the limit of our vision."*

It is true that our vision as human beings is very limited. It is only when feelings which are inexplicable take us over that we begin to dig a little deeper into ourselves and see a little further than we saw before.

I seem to be going through another cycle, Stephen, just when I thought I was winning! You father's absence is not helping. I had got used to him being here after his long trek abroad. I was so wrapped up in my own sorrow and other people seemed to get in the way. Then there was a stage when I needed your father to hold on to and we both gained great comfort from each other's presence. Sleeping was something I looked forward to because I could relax with this warm person next to me. Now he will be away until July and I am having to learn to cope alone again. Inside me there is a greater strength, but physically I am exhausted. There seem to be so many demands on my time that I wonder if I will ever be able to cope. I really need to get away but as the days go by the chances of that happening lessen.

Many requests have arrived for astrological charts, from as far away as Africa. I don't know how they manage to get hold of my name for it must be two years now since I have advertised.

Then there is my presentation for the education conference; it is so strange how things happen. I was asked to fill in a questionnaire from the Open Unversity, just after you died. There were pages of questions about my experience as a student and what I felt about the courses I had taken. I wrote back a letter saying that I did not believe in questionnaires — packaging people into boxes. Pages and pages I wrote, going on about the education system and how little anyone really cared about young people, or the crises they went through at University. I did go a bit over the top, but I felt much better afterwards! Weeks later I received a letter suggesting I attended an international conference about the problems of first-year University students, as it was felt I had some personal experience to offer.

You know how strongly I feel about the lack of communication between the system and young people, so I had no alternative but to accept. From my discussions with your brothers and many others, I know there is a great desire to 'fit in'. I am beginning to realise that it is more than just a desire, it is a sheer necessity for them. What a pity you did not discuss this with each other instead of each young person thinking that he or she was the only one who did not fit in. You felt that way, Stephen, but, you see, so did everyone else — they just said nothing to you about it, nor for that matter to anyone.

'No other option open' is the continual response I am getting from the students filling in records of their experiences. Of course I see that now. You had no real choice. You had been groomed for academic study and if you did not concentrate on that, the system did not provide an alternative path. I remember how intent you were on putting the required effort in and doing well. I feel so sad that you were not around to reap the rewards of all your efforts.

I hope I am successful at the conference in persuading the 'powers-that-be' that young, able people need a great deal of help and assistance in their first year at University. I am discovering that so many drop out, or get involved with drugs, or take their lives. Even those who finish successfully talk about the traumas and anxieties of their first year. There is no real communication between the schools and the universities, and the 'culture shock' caused by the step between the two establishments just proves to be too great for some. If *you* had not died, I doubt very much whether I would have been asked to attend.

I am going there to help people like you, Stephen, and hopefully make a dent in 'the system'. The students' path has to be made smoother because they are as special as any one else, and as much in need of a spokesman for their cause. I realise I am only one person and can do very little, but if I only plant one seed — who knows? It may be the right seed in the right soil. I owe it to you and other young people like you to be there.

I received my second newsletter from The Compassionate Friends, an organisation to help parents whose children have died. The first newsletter included many tragic deaths of young people but there was not one example of suicide. I cried reading all the letters and poems. There is so much

61

sadness and loneliness when young people die. I did not really feel part of any of this because they had not died as you had died. However in the second newsletter there was an item from someone who had lost a daughter through suicide. She had been told to take it a day at a time, but after a year she did not feel any better. She requested help and advice. I feel I must write something to be included in the Summer edition, just to let her know she is not alone.

The Compassionate Friends are thinking of setting up a separate section, solely for parents whose children have died in this way. They already have a section for parents of children who have been murdered. I understand the need for different sections, because you can only really identify with someone who has gone through the same experience. Counsellors were mentioned, as a better idea than just commiserating with each other. I am not sure about this. I cannot help feeling that, in the end, each of us has to come to terms with our loss in our own way.

I feel something good must come out of all this pain and, although I have a deep understanding of the suffering of those left behind, the only way this suffering can be creatively channelled is for these same people to do something, however small, for the young people of this world.

The Compassionate Friends is a wonderful organisation, and has helped thousands of people. There will always be a need for such organisations to help suffering humanity. Some of those who have been helped by The Compassionate Friends go on to help others who are going through the same experience. There will be others who feel they cannot achieve this but who, like me, feel they must make use of this horrendous experience. It cannot possibly be forgotten; even to try to obliterate it from their minds could be a serious mistake, leading perhaps to other kinds of problems. But they need to find a way to channel the effects of what they have gone through and, hopefully, to grow through it.

In your letter, Stephen, you said "I hope Mum recovers to conquer the world." I really did not know what you meant at the time, except that you hoped I would go on to do something of value. Recovering takes time and I am not 'there' yet. Recovering also means coming to terms with losing you. This does not mean forgetting, but remembering and turning despair into hope. On occasions, I look through the photograph album which I made up of you from the time when you were a tiny child to the last photograph you had taken, three weeks before you died. I still cry, but I am not shouting "Why him? Why him?" any more, or "Why did you do this to me, Stephen?" Now I say, "Yes, I remember that holiday in the Lakes a few years ago. You were so happy with all your brothers, walking, climbing and eating like a horse." Sometimes I say, "So why did it have to end?" but then I turn the page to recall another stage of your life.

Every night I ask God to look after *you* and to help *me* become stronger and less concerned with myself. When things get too much, I put the whole lot in His hands and accept the consequences. Without knowing it, I must have always been a believer because without this God, who has given me an inner strength I did not know I possessed, I would not be alive today. I really believed that a death such as yours would end my life, as it was the worst possible thing I could imagine happening to me. I know you did not take your own life to prove anything, but wherever you are you will know that I have gained a strength that was never in me until now. I am still recovering, Stephen, but I feel the stirrings of something deeper. I am far more positive than I used to be, and less afraid of other people's reactions.

I have never enjoyed being at the mercy of a social system, and often remained quiet when I should have spoken out. Now there does not seem to be any real need for such diplomacy.

Today I put the house up for sale. I know it is time to go from here. But it would be nice to have more energy and interest in it all. I have to admit it — I'm missing you, Stephen, in spite of the fact that you will never really go. As I move around the house, getting rid of all the rubbish that goes with moving, I feel a very deep sense of loss and isolation. Now that I am more in control of myself, I am aware of the grief. Some months ago it was just an intense pain; now it is an intense loneliness, with the realisation that you have gone from this world.

Your father appears to be quite happy in Abu Dhabi, although he does not like being alone. If his contract is renewable, he will make arrangements for Andrew and me to live out there for a while. At the moment I would welcome a new start, but in a way I feel I am being forced to put my house in order first. There are so many things to do. Streams of potential buyers have been calling to see the house. That means that I have to keep the place organised. I try not to show it, but I feel myself getting rather irritated by their presence, especially when they pause in the room where you used to sleep. I feel they are intruding. I can see their eyes looking round disdainfully at the lack of material comforts — comments such as "I see it's not centrally heated" and "we would of course have to rip this kitchen out and start again." It's our house they're talking about, Stephen, the house where we had so much fun and laughter, the house where so many young people came because they felt at home here. It was your home for most of your life. You grew up here and in the end never wanted to leave. Who the hell are these people?

We have planning permission now to convert the house into two flats, so I will probably let it go to a builder who will completely change its character. I don't mind the builders looking around. They think in terms of living space — so down to earth! They never even notice that two thousand books are packed into the front room, all read at some time or another by one of us. Yes, I hope a builder buys it; I can cope with that.

I received a 'phone call at 3.00 a.m. this morning from a travel firm. "Are you the parent of a young man who travelled to Paris yesterday?" asked the voice. I took a long time to answer. Brian was on a sales trip with his firm and there could not be many reasons they were ringing me at this time in the morning. He was either in trouble or had been in an accident. "There has been an accident," said the voice. Before they gave me any further information — which must have only been seconds in time — I had him dead and buried and was putting another vase on the grave. "He's OK," said the voice. "He was lucky. The bus he was travelling in went through a level crossing and was hit by a train. The people in front are dead but the remaining seven are all right."

I rang the hospital in Paris where he was spending the night because of shock, and he was fine. It was then that I realised that the first cut is the deepest, and in a weird and strange way your death had given me some kind of inoculation. I do not want any of your brothers to die and I would grieve for them as I do you, but the blow can never be the same again. If Brian had died, I would have recalled the pain of death again, but it would be a remembering and not something new to me. At the time, other people said they did not see how I could have survived a second death in so short a time. How could I tell them that it was the survival of the first death which was the miracle? They did not experience it and so do not really understand. I thanked them for their concern but did not try to explain.

Brian understood; no words were necessary for him. The morning you died, each one of us had looked death in the face, with the realisation that one day we would all experience the end of our life on this earth. It is not something we dwell on, or even bother to think about, until we are faced with so close an encounter. We are not going to live on this

65

earth for ever and maybe today is our last day so there is no point in wasting it. I asked Brian what was passing through his mind when he felt the impact of the train. "Just pain," he said. "I was waiting for the pain and I had a feeling that I'd been here before."

If anything had happened to him, the cross I am carrying would have increased in weight — and I am not looking for heavier crosses to carry. However, it is my cross, no one else's; and it would not have been given to me unless I was capable of carrying it. I would not exchange it either because there are far heavier crosses than mine.

There was a major accident at a nuclear power station in Russia today. Many were killed and many contaminated. The dust cloud has moved across Scandinavia, raising the levels of radioactivity to a hundred times the normal level. Other countries are complaining about the light water reactor used by the Russians. They say it is unsafe and this method has, in fact, been rejected by all Western countries.

I am happy to see that the West is offering help to Russia, to assist them in sorting out ways of containing the problem. Why does it need a disaster to bring people together and make them realise that we have more things in common than we have apart? We cannot afford 'accidents' which pose a threat to the survival of the whole world. I am not very happy about living in a nuclear age, but I realise there is very little I can do about it. The knowledge which enables us to use nuclear power will always be with us but I do wish the political leaders of the world would get together and put a complete freeze on the build-up of weapons and find other ways of producing energy.

Time, I feel, is running out. Before long, there will be no choice.

I travelled to the north of England to attend the wedding of the young man who stayed with us for a few weeks in the autumn of 1984. Do you remember how we welcomed his entrance into our lives? We were feeling pretty low at the time; your father was still in Saudi Arabia and Mark, whom you were always so close to, had just left for a teaching post in East Africa. This young man, with all his enthusiasm, brought laughter and living back into our lives. I remember the fun we all had playing ten-pin bowling on Saturdays. He hated losing, which he usually did, but he took it all in good part as we notched up strike after strike. I remember you were very happy during those weeks and became completely extroverted as you hotly debated world issues. You really came out of your shell and I was beginning to see a vibrant, positive, confident young man. He came to your funeral and shared with us the sad hopelessness at the terrible loss of your young life.

So, Stephen, I went to his wedding to share with him his joy in a new beginning. It was a grand occasion and I was warmly welcomed. Unfortunately, your father could not be there as he will not be home until July. I missed him terribly and, in spite of the sincerity of everyone, I felt very much alone. I joined in the celebration wholeheartedly and it wasn't until the late evening, when I closed the door of my room, that I realised what an enormous, but necessary effort, it had all been. I made some coffee and cried continually for about two hours. This letting go had broken down all my control and my tears were a blessed release. Finally, exhausted, I fell asleep. This road to recovery is not going to be easy, but I felt that I had taken at least one step.

May continues and I am finding myself becoming more and more involved with the outside world. There is a great reluctance to do this on my part but it is as though I am being given no option. Constant reminders about the conference I will be attending keep dropping through the letterbox so that I have to spend time getting all the facts into some semblance of order. In addition, I have opted to go on a weekend in Manchester with members of The Compassionate Friends. Meeting people who have gone through a similar experience may give me some idea how far I have travelled since that terrible morning when you left us, Stephen. I am not looking forward to going, but I feel I must.

I am constantly in the company of estate agents and prospective buyers as I try to complete this house move. The house is slowly emptying as I get rid of beds, furniture and the accumulated assortment of twelve years' residence here. I feel every article I throw away is a little bit of my past. Next week your bed will be going, and most of your clothes have been distributed amongst your brothers. You wanted to leave all you had to your family so I have given Martin the cassette player and finally parted with your watch. Your blazer hangs in the cupboard under the stairs, still containing the smell of you. I'm not brave enough to get rid of it yet. Your favourite green sweater and your box of keepsakes are still with me. I cannot imagine ever getting rid of them. The cards you received on your eighteenth birthday are on the top. The one from Mark has a poem in it which reads:

> *Without stirring abroad, one can know the whole world.*
> *Without looking out of the window, one can see the way to*
>   *heaven.*
> *The further one goes, the less one knows.*
> *Therefore the sage knows without having to stir,*
>   *identifies without having to see,*
>   *accomplishes without having to act.*
>
> *Tao Te Ching*

You always knew that, didn't you, Stephen — the grass is not greener over the hill. All you ever had and really wanted was here. At least I can understand that much. Six intelligent, though zany, brothers, provided all the fun, conversation and laughter you needed. The outside world could only offer you lessons to learn and I can see now what a frightening new experience this was for you.

I know you did not survive it, Stephen, and you paid such a high price. You were never a coward; in fact I would say that you were really trying to make an adult decision, except that you were not mature enough to make it. You must have felt so lost and lonely and unable to see that you had only to ask and we would have been able to help. None of us was aware that you had any real problem. Nevertheless I cannot opt out of responsibility. I should have been more positive in helping you to secure a temporary job for the summer months so that you would have been busy and paid less attention to yourself. I thought I was doing you a favour in allowing you to relax before you started on your course. My fault was my over-protectiveness. It would have been far more difficult for me to see you working long hours at some spare-time job when I knew how exhausted you were after the examinations.

It is so difficult being a parent in these stressful days. There are pressures from almost every area and the advancement of technology brings disasters into our living room almost as soon as they happen. Although the television set can be a great source of learning and pleasure, it can also brainwash us with constant information about one disaster after another, so that our minds become over-loaded and we just cannot take any more. There is pressure from the schools to see that our children work hard and receive good examination grades to make their job prospects more promising; more pressure when they achieve good grades and remain unemployed because there are not enough jobs to go around. Disasters from nuclear accidents cause worry about the environment. Will our children have a future? Government departments grow bigger and bigger and more bureaucratic, so that we have to fill in reams and reams of forms before we can get an education grant or a rate rebate. Hospitals and doctors' surgeries are so understaffed that we have to wait hours, sometimes weeks, even months for attention.

Add to this the increasing violence and crime, and constant pressures from charitable organisations begging help for those who are even worse off than we are and is it any wonder that we are not flowing with optimism? Our children are lost as we are lost, and at times I feel we are passing on our anxiety to them. In spite of all, there is an optimistic streak within me and, because I love my children, I continually encourage them to strive for a better world.

You always admired my fighting spirit, Stephen, and I knew there were times when you were willing me to succeed against all odds. I felt you wanted me to obtain some tangible reward. I remember that when I finally received my BA degree, you were really enthusiastic about my success, especially since I had to fit in all the studying in any spare hours I had. The fact that I managed to obtain the degree was reward enough for me, but I felt you wanted to see something more; some high-flying position or material success. Perhaps you thought it was wasted effort or that I had missed out in some way.

There are days now when I wish I had gone out there and achieved something tangible, just for your sake, so that you could see some end-result. It might have made your journey easier because you would have been able to see some hope in your life; some reward for all your efforts. More than anything, I wanted all seven of you to be happy and successful. I really tried to help and encourage you along the way and it is only now the realisation dawns — that you wanted exactly the same for me. You wanted to give, more than you wanted to receive, and I gave you very little opportunity to do that.

It is a little late for wisdom, Stephen, but as I look around this house now I am constantly reminded of conversations we had together. When I needed to get away some times, you would say "I'll look after Andrew for the weekend," and I would reply "Oh no, Stephen, you're too young and it's not your responsibility." Perhaps that is exactly what you needed and wanted, some responsibility.

I am sure every mother, under the circumstances, digs and digs and finds so many areas where she went wrong. We aim at perfection, which is impossible. In your heart I know you attach no blame whatsoever to me — quite the contrary — but it matters what I feel about myself. That is why I am moving from this house, Stephen; not to forget you, but to stop this self-persecution and to create a little hope and optimism somewhere else; a new beginning, in fact.

Although I think of you every day, and probably always will, the intervals between the sad reminders are getting longer. In earlier months when the bad times were getting farther apart, they were heavier when they arrived. Now, with an even longer gap, they are like thunderbolts. I have physically to curl up in a ball to take the sudden surge of feeling when it blasts in at me. I begin to wonder if there will be some kind of finale and whether or not I can handle it when it arrives. Though it is not a good thing to dwell on this terrible experience, the daily grieving is a necessary part of my survival.

Some people recommend that I fill my life with as many interests as possible and, by co-incidence, I have been forced to do this. However, it is not necessarily a good thing because I am being denied my daily grief. This has the effect of 'putting it on ice' as it were, so that it builds and builds and finally explodes. Gentle daily grieving is much kinder to my spirit than monthly massive explosions. From now on, no matter how many calls there are on my time, I will lay aside a period of quiet contemplation every day, just to communicate with you, Stephen. My sadness is still new and I can still say 'this time last year he was here', so I will get upset and other people will just have to cope with that. I am attempting to survive the most devastating experience of my life, with no real guidelines on how it is to be done. Like any addiction — we are addicted to our children, whether we know it or not — there is no cure. You always have to take it one day

71

at a time. So I will do that, in my own way and in my own time.

Mark has been teaching for a short time in this country; a far cry from his teaching days in Africa! As you very well know Stephen, he is a wonderful communicator of facts — a born teacher, and there are not many of them around. He enjoyed preparing interesting lessons and was often rewarded by personal thanks from the pupils. Sadly, the 'system' did not share his enthusiasm. Controlling children and keeping them quiet was the major priority; teaching was secondary to that.

He learned a great deal and refused to become part of that system, happily putting up with the noise and refusing to shout or become aggressive. He would have no part, either, in administering corporal punishment nor in condoning it and, as he put it, 'refused to teach under a veil of fear'. He is now preparing himself for a postgraduate course which will enable him to teach in colleges of further education. I am sure he has made the right decision because the students there will be 'volunteers', as against children who *have* to be there. There will be no need for 'control' and he can happily get on with what he loves best — sharing ideas with like-minded people.

June

By a stroke of fate I spent three days and three nights alone at the end of May. Paul had moved into his new flat. Mark and Brian were away visiting friends and young Andrew was off camping. I really did not like the idea of being alone; in fact, since I was married almost thirty years ago, I have only once been totally alone in the house for more than one day — one of the perks of having a large family! I felt very lost and thought about you more than ever. I turned the television on and many lights, just to give the place a feeling of life. I cooked meals for myself but when it came to eating the food, I found I could not manage it. All I could see were those faces around the table. I really could not believe that only five years ago, there were nine of us sitting around that table, chatting, laughing and arguing. I thought about the time, three years ago, when the family was reduced to four for a while and how much we enjoyed the brief respite. At least we could get into the bathroom without queuing, and spoil ourselves on occasions with cordon bleu cooking.

As I sat there looking at the empty spaces, I realised how much I missed those happy times and how I hated being alone. I thought of the many old people who eat alone every day; they must also have memories of happier times. I cried for quite a while and then I thought of your happy smiling face and your voice in my head urging me to drag myself out of this depressing pit. I put on some happy sixties music and drank a toast to my sons for all the happy times they had given me. I even dressed up and went out to visit friends, just to talk about the weather and holidays and ordinary things. I know you found sadness hard to cope with and could not bear to see anyone unhappy, so because I know you are out there somewhere, I am making the effort for you, Stephen.

I went up to visit relatives in the North of England for a few days. Unfortunately it was raining and misty and not at all like the beginning of June. Still, the welcome was warm and the company a much-needed blessing. I even visited my old school and whilst I was walking along the road I trod so often as a young girl, I had the feeling, just for a second or two, that the past, present and future had all rolled into one. I realised with amazing clarity that life is continually changing and that nothing is really permanent.

73

We cannot hold on to things; we can just catch the experience as it flies past. The experiences remain somewhere in our memory, which is why the past feels a part of the present and the future will still feel a part of the past. In essence it is all really one. It is just because we become so earthbound that we think we can attach ourselves to things and people, and create a static form of life. We are born and we die and nothing any of us does can alter that. However, there are beautiful experiences along the way and one of the greatest is surely the joy of knowing and loving people.

We now have a buyer for the house, so getting rid of useless articles has become a daily task. As I empty drawers and cupboards I keep coming across things belonging to you. Yesterday I found two of your third-form maths books and the clipper board you used on a biology field-trip. My first thought was "Will he want to keep them, or shall I throw them away?" Just as quickly I remembered that you were not here to ask, so I would have to decide to throw them away or keep them; it is so very difficult, Stephen! I feel I am letting you down somehow if I throw your personal things away, because I know how you used to keep things — a 'Steptoe', like your father! I would never have thrown away your bed, except that it really was at the end of its days. Andrew loved to sleep in it because it belonged to you and we shared many tears when we saw it stacked outside, ready for removal.

The snooker table has also gone. Do you remember the Christmas you shared this present with Martin? You must have been about thirteen; only six years ago. You were always very good at the game yourself and from the moment that table appeared in the house it was never out of use. There were competitions and tournaments, and the dining table was invisible most weekends.

I remember lying in bed most Saturdays and stuffing my ears with cotton wool to cut out the sound of clacking snooker balls. So many young people came to play on it, even when they owned a far superior piece of equipment themselves. It wasn't just the table, was it? They came for the company and the lively discussions, and the freedom which you find in large families. Gallons of tea and quantities of toasted sandwiches were consumed during these noisy, happy times. The table was worn out, and when we put it on to the skip Andrew chopped it into pieces, but not before he had cut out a piece of the green baize. He brought it into the house, neatly folded, and said, "This is to remind me of Stephen. Put it into his box with all his other things." You were his brother, his teacher and his very dearest friend. He loved you.

I always thought that when I left this house I would be enthusiastic about it; such an old house and so much work. However, I am finding it a very painful experience. Somehow it signifies the end of an era which can never be repeated.

How I hate beginnings and endings. I can manage the bit in-between, but beginnings and endings tear me apart. There is no flow; no balance; the future looks like an empty vessel with no one steering it and the enormous effort required to live just in the present is physically and emotionally draining. Eventually I will have to steer that vessel to calmer waters and begin again. For me, a new order will have to be created from the ashes of the old one and I pray daily that I will have the courage to make it.

Andrew is just a child, but he is great teacher. When he is asked how many brothers he has, he always says 'six'. I know you will like that, Stephen. You see, to Andrew death is just another state, not an annihilation. When he was born, he had six brothers and for him that will always be so. He lives life to the full and when he does talk to me about you he says "When I get a sad thought, I change it to a happy one." How simple and how difficult unless you are a child! God must protect the very young and the very old; he gives them so much wisdom. Perhaps the time in between is just a testing period for the very simple acceptance of life.

We are now in the middle of June and the weather has turned exceptionally hot. I recall last June, when you had finished your 'A' levels. You came in through the kitchen door after your final examination and literally jumped for joy. "I've finished, I've finished," you sang, "no more school and I can lie in every morning." You made yourself two enormous toasted sandwiches and the usual large mug of tea. The scene is so vivid and you looked so contented and happy. Eight weeks from that day you were dead, Stephen.

When I think of that, it is almost impossible to believe that it ever happened. I can only live for today now. I make plans and arrangements which hopefully will materialise, but in effect I only live for today. There is nothing else to be really sure about, except now; neither is there any use worrying about tomorrow because today, tomorrow is a mystery.

Martin has just completed the final papers for his Chemistry degree, and Graduation Day will be on 10th July. This takes place in the middle of the Education Conference I am attending, so after reading my paper on the 9th, I intend to take the train to Manchester, in time for the ceremony. We do not, of course, know the outcome of the final examination until the end of June, so there is no point in making concrete plans until then.

An item of news in the papers this week was the death of a young woman at Oxford University. She was found dead at a party, after the finals, where she had taken some drug and eventually choked to death. Her father is a Government Minister and comes from a fairly wealthy family, so the story was in all the national papers. Actually, Stephen, I could think no further than the sadness her parents are experiencing. They are having the kind of time I experienced last year and, no matter how wealthy they are, they cannot escape the pain and sorrow at the loss of their young daughter in such circumstances. Perhaps, in time, her father may take a personal interest in the too-easy availability of drugs to young people and use his position to get something done about the problem.

There are many sad and lonely young people at University and scores of them have died under similar circumstances. The whole educational system of this country needs a thorough overhaul and I feel the pressure will have to come from the parents who have suffered the loss of a child through the bureaucratic rigidity of a system that is out-of-date, uncaring and has far too many chiefs and nowhere near enough indians. I recall your words again, Stephen, in the note you left when you died. "It all started when I visited the University and realised I would not fit in."

I have just returned from a weekend in Manchester, organised by The Compassionate Friends. It was the first residential weekend they had arranged for bereaved parents. The weather took a turn for the better; in fact temperatures soared into the eighties. A girls' residential college, belonging to Manchester University, was chosen to accommodate us all. It was also the annual general meeting of the organisation, although I felt that most of the people there were more interested in meeting other parents who had gone through the painful sorrow of losing a child.

I went there with a lady who had been a member for quite a while. She had lost a son in a motor-cycle accident many years before, but said that she liked to keep in touch with the friends she had made over the years. I felt at home as soon as we arrived at the college. The accommodation was very simple and there was an air of peace about the place.

It was a Catholic college run by Sister Eileen; she and her sister-nuns took excellent care of us throughout the weekend.

There were a number of odd coincidences during that week-end. I was born in Manchester, so in a sense I was going home. When I attended Mass on Sunday morning, I realised that the church was the place where I met your father for the first time. He had only been there once in his life before and so had I, and we never went there again. As I walked towards the church, I passed the hospital where you were born, Stephen. Even though we had moved away from the area in our early married years, we had returned so that your father could complete a third year in College. Then I met a woman who was actually a nurse at that very hospital, during that period. She mentioned that she could possibly have delivered you. I did feel very much at peace in this place.

I met some lovely people and it was such a relief not to have to make the effort to keep your death out of the conversation. We did not concentrate on the sadness we all felt but we did share our experiences, how they had affected us and how other people, outside the situation, had reacted. Once again death was the opposite side of the coin to birth. When you are expecting a child and it gets towards the end of the pregnancy, people say "How long is it now before the baby will be born?" When you lose that child people say "How long is it since it happened?"

I was asked this question so many times over the weekend. Just as it takes nine months to have a child, it appears there are time elements in bereavement too. Under twelve months is considered definitely 'early days', and I was in this category, Stephen. Three years is considered 'coming to terms with'. Any longer is dealt with by the remark: "You now realise it will never go away and that you have to live again and accept the added burden you have to carry." However, just as the birth of a child varies in time — the pregnancy could be nine, eight or seven months, or even earlier — so does the time of grieving vary. I met people who had not moved out

78

of the first stage after seven years, and others who were on the third stage after less than twelve months.

Nature cannot be packaged and I feel bereavement certainly cannot be put into 'stages of grief'. There are so many different factors involved. When you died, Stephen, you were in your own home and so were most of your family. We all expected to get up that morning and see you as usual. You weren't ill, you weren't in any dangerous situation and, as far as we knew, you would be with us as usual. The shock of finding you dead that morning and the realisation that you had taken your own life gave us all such an agonising shock that we responded like dying animals in pain. We could not 'put on an act' to make each other feel better; we were completely incapable of doing anything other than responding to this nightmare. Because of this, we were always able to talk about your death openly with each other. If anything could be termed 'good' about all of this, it must have been a blessing that we were not given the chance to let any conditioning prevent us from responding to losing you. We could share what we really felt at that moment in time. No outsider, such as the doctor or the police who were in the house, could help but see the pain of a family in deep distress. Looking back, I am glad that it happened in the way it did because it allowed us all, in the months that followed, an easier release of our buried emotions. We could grieve for you openly, with no embarrassment.

I am telling you this, Stephen, because while I was away this weekend, I heard of so many people who were still stuck in the first grieving stage, because their children had refused to talk about the death of their brother or sister and in some cases cannot even mention their name again. They may have been away from home when the child died, and so they were given the time to put on the 'brave face' mask felt to be demanded by the social order of this age. When I see the faces of these parents, I feel I want to go up to the children and say "Weep with your parents, hold them and share with them the loss that binds you so closely. Forget what is expected of you by the world! Allow your real emotions to surface

79

and share them with your family; that will give them the freedom to move on to the final stage of grief."

God wasn't mentioned much during the weekend, but when asked I told them about my own experience, when I begged Him for help on the day of your funeral. I was patted on the head by one person 'cured' of bereavement (a fourth stage which as far as I am aware does not exist) with the remark "Well, I expect it made you feel better." Actually it did not make me feel better. I felt just as bad. I begged for help because, for the first time in my life, I realised that I was no longer in control and that I would need a 'higher order' to help me. I cannot imagine why I ever felt I was in control but, just like everyone else, I did.

Before you died, Stephen, I really believed that all my children would grow up and be happy, that I was one of the lucky ones and life would be a 'happy ever after' story. When I heard about other children taking their lives I used to feel sad and think "I hope that never happens to me," but then I used to forget it and because I sincerely believed that if such a terrible thing did happen, I would just die from the experience and so I would not be around to have to cope with it. When you died in this way and I was still here, I really could not cope with the pain. I delayed asking God for His help for a week because I felt so guilty at having played the role of God for so long, I had lived my life so far believing that I knew my own limitations, believing that I knew which experiences I could cope with and which I could not. Even in the week after you died and I was still around, I had thoughts that I had just made an error of judgement, in the sense that I was stronger than I felt and so eventually I would learn to cope. Still in control, you see, Stephen! I really believed I was in control.

The moment I left the house on the day of your funeral, I knew I was incapable of coping. Still I thought that, with human help, I would be all right. I hung on to your father and to each of your brothers in turn, but I was still incapable. With very little hope remaining, I made a last final effort. I took hold of Andrew's hand, a child's hand. I was asking a child, who was himself so confused and grief-stricken, to give me the strength to cope. I felt so ashamed. I let go of his hand and shuffled down the church, holding on to every bench along the way. When I sat down and looked at the crucifix, I knew there was only one way. I told Him I could not take any more and I would have to pass this burden over to Him. I was neither dead nor alive, just in some kind of pain vacuum. I begged Him to help me move out of it. Slowly, I began to feel physically in control of my body again and I found myself singing the hymns and saying the prayers of the Requiem Mass. The heaviness of the sadness was indescribable, but now it was not unbearable because I knew He was helping me carry this cross.

So, to the person who patted me on the head, I would say "It wasn't a matter of making me 'feel better', but a realisation that I now had a heavier burden to carry. I was going to have to learn how to live on afterwards. There was a difference now, however. Some force, some higher order, some deity would help me along the way. Call it what you will; hang it under the banner of Christianity, Buddhism, Islam, Judaism or any other religion. I call it God because I asked Him and He answered."

I gained a great deal from going to this weekend and I have to thank the people who organised everything and allowed me this experience. My only criticism would be that far too much time was spent in meetings and minutes, which left less time for people to interact spontaneously with each other.

A separate group for the parents of children who had taken their own lives was set up. There was quite a number of these parents there, and I gained some comfort talking to them. I realised I had not been singled out for this particular pain. There were discussions about counsellors and the possibility of training such people. I feel that once you create the position of a counsellor and a person to be counselled, you create a hierarchy. The counsellor becomes the one who has

81

all the answers — the higher position; the counselled becomes the one who is seeking answers to questions — the lower position. Far better to organise gatherings of people in an empathetic environment and allow them to counsel each other without even being conscious of doing it. When they have gained all they need from such encounters, they can hopefully move on to become involved in helping others. Out of these tragic events, something positive and meaningful could emerge.

When I returned from this weekend with The Compassionate Friends, there was only a week before I attended the Conference in Newcastle. I must admit, Stephen, that I was thoroughly exhausted. Perhaps it was because I had listened to so many sad stories and seen so much pain in people's faces. All I know is that I almost collapsed that week and on Friday I began to suffer intense pain in my ears. It grew so bad that I had to attend the local hospital as an out-patient that weekend. Depression overtook me when I thought of all the time and effort I had put into my Conference paper and now perhaps I would be unable to deliver it. I decided once again to leave it in the hands of a higher order; if I was meant to attend, then I would recover.

Apart from hospital visits, I spent most of the weekend in bed and by Sunday afternoon I was free from any pain. I packed a suitcase and left early on Monday morning for the Conference. Travelling up by train, I got into conversation with a young girl on her way to look over Durham University. She was seventeen and in the first year of her 'A' levels, and she was obviously extremely nervous. It was a very hot day and she sat there in a thick anorak, clutching a large weekend bag. At my suggestion she put the bag between the seats and took off her anorak.

We chatted together all the way to York, where she had to change trains. She was very worried about choosing a University and went on to explain that she had been given very little help in this direction. I told her about the Conference I was attending and all the case histories I had in my bag regarding the problems in the first year at University. She confirmed everything the students had said about this particular stage in their education, which gave me renewed confidence in my own paper. I was nervous about the part I had to play, mainly because I knew I would be the odd one out — the only person not involved in higher education as an employee.

On my arrival at Newcastle Polytechnic I was given a folder containing a full programme of events, a name tag and a blue satin ribbon with the word 'Presenter' painted on it. I really felt like an intruder in this educational hierarchy, especially when people came up to me and asked "Who are you?". Before I could explain myself, they would peer at my name tag, and if they were British would say "Ah! Open University — didn't know they were presenting anything!" I was flying under the banner of the Open University as an ex-student, my partner being the Research Educationalist who had invited me to attend.

I was beginning to wish I had filled in his questionnaire as an ex-student, then the strange twist of events which had followed and was responsible for my presence at this Conference would not have occurred. I had constantly to remind myself that I was here because of you, Stephen, and for future students who were finding our educational system so difficult to cope with.

There were many Americans at the Conference and their open and extroverted approach stirred up something in me that I had not felt since I was a child — my enthusiasm! My confidence was certainly in need of a boost if I was ever going to make a success of presenting this paper; it had already been undermined by the comment of one of the organisers — "Could you please be careful that your ethnographic small-scale approach doesn't tip over into mere anecdote; your number of cases is very small and there could be some glaring holes in your argument"!

The Establishment need not have worried nor, for that matter, need I. It was the only paper with actual case histories, and the Research man and I presented our paper to one of the largest audiences of the week, which was an amazing feat in itself since there were sixteen sessions going on at exactly the same time. The people present were glad to talk about real people with real problems, and there was much agreement from both sides of the Atlantic on many of the conclusions.

I never mentioned you in my paper, Stephen, but it was a relief to find that one of the main areas of attention was the enormous gap between school and university which had resulted in my paper, 'Culture Shock', being presented. All the students and University Admissions Officers to whom I had talked mentioned this huge leap. I had always been aware, when your brothers went to University, that there were problems but it was only when you died and I went into the whole educational process in detail that I realised how tremendous these problems are.

Many areas were discussed and I gave everyone a copy of the case histories. There were counsellors, chaplains and administrative officers present, and I can only hope that they went back to their schools and colleges with a greater determination to help these young, able people.

I left the Conference on Thursday morning to attend Martin's degree ceremony. Yes, Stephen, he gained his Honours Degree and I was there to see him walk up in his ermine and pink striped hood to receive it. I looked around at all the students, who had spent three years or more working for this piece of paper, and at their parents, dressed appropriately for the day. Many, like me, had travelled long distances to be there and so I found it very sad that the Vice-Chancellor did not even address the students collectively and congratulate them for the amount of effort they had made. Their names were called out very quickly and it reminded me of an academic farming process. Quite lengthy periods were spent honouring elderly graduates, talking about their past lives and even mentioning their wonderful gardens! I cannot imagine what the students felt like, except perhaps that it had nothing at all to do with them.

This was the University you would have attended, Stephen, and if you also had the feelings which I experienced that day then I can fully understand why you felt you would not fit in. In fact, I could hear your voice in my head saying "You see what I mean, Mum?"!

July

Your father will be returning from Abu Dhabi on July 17 but so far there is no news of his going back or of our going out there. John and Lorraine's first child is now a week over-due and we all have the feeling that it will arrive on the day your father returns. Andrew and I are staying overnight with my brother, as the flight comes in at five o'clock in the morning.

It is fortunate there are so many things happening as I am beginning to feel very depressed, the closer it gets to the anniversary of your death. I have always been able to say, this time last year he was doing so-and-so; soon I will not be able to say that any more. I still find Sunday evenings hard to take, because the last time I spoke to you was on a Sunday evening. Strange how I can still remember the events and conversations of the last weekend with you so clearly.

On Saturday, your father was painting the house and I was trying to sort out the garden. You came out and said "Cup of tea, Mum?" I said "Oh!, lovely, Stephen," and sat down on the grass. You brought out mugs of tea for all of us and your father came down the ladder to drink his. "Which is mine?" he asked. Trying to keep your face straight, you said "Yours is the one with the fly in it". We all burst out laughing, including your father. You took over the hoeing from me,

85

showing me a quick way to do it, and we all spent a daft, happy hour together.

On Sunday John came round to ask his father's assistance in repairing his car. It was a terribly wet and windy day; most of the summer had been like that. You got up quite late that day and seemed sad that you had missed most of John's visit. I have often wondered since then if you were going to talk with him about your University choice. As he is the eldest, you always thought of him as your 'little father'. I have to stop myself thinking about that possibility, especially since he chose to do his degree at a Polytechnic and I realise, now, that would have been a better choice for you. Who knows what a difference that conversation might have made?

During the lunch-time of that day, your father, John and I went out for a drink. I had spent much of the morning doing an astrological chart, and when we were chatting at the pub, John made a remark about the change in you over the last two years and how you had given up most of your sporting activities. I said it was probably due to your 'A' level studies and we were making an effort to get you back into the stream of things again. You had been playing tennis with Paul and no doubt soon you would be feeling more like your old self. The conversation carried on and suddenly I remarked that, astrologically, this was probably the worst week of the whole year and that if we could get over this week, we could get over anything. John asked laughingly who was it a bad week for and I replied "For everyone, for everyone."

The strange thing is that I must have made this comment to everyone and indicated that it was certainly not the week to make decisions. You were the only person to whom I did not mention it. Although you always took my astrological trends with tongue-in-cheek, you did not dismiss them entirely. I wonder why I never got around to telling you about this indication?

I spent the evening of that day writing a long letter to Mark in Africa, while you watched a comedy on television with your father. I remember writing to Mark that I was suddenly beginning to feel less depressed about things and that when this week was over, I was sure things were going to be different. I asked if you wanted to enclose a letter to Mark and you said "Oh, I don't feel like writing now, I'll write next week." I replied "You're always putting things off, Stephen." How I wish I had never made that remark. Perhaps you were also thinking of putting off ending your own life and that remark made you more determined. I pray that was not so, but I will never know the answer to that.

Your father and I went out for a while and I changed into a black skirt and waistcoat. It was only the evening before that I had remarked I never wore black in the summer unless I was going to a funeral. When we returned, you had a bit of a sniffle and I could not find any hay-fever pills. In the end I gave you an aspirin and said I would get the hay-fever pills the following morning. Your father made some supper and we chatted about your brothers. Then your father went to bed and because I wasn't all that tired, I was going to suggest making some coffee. For some reason I did not do that. I seemed to stand at the door for ages, talking to you. You admitted you were not tired as you had got up late. I began to talk about tomorrow and getting into some form of routine. I said "Don't stay up late will you, Stephen, I don't like leaving you here on your own." "No, I won't stay up late," you said.

Only you know the rest. Those few hours between me leaving you and Paul finding you dead remain a mystery to us. Knowing you, we can only conclude that you spent no time at all thinking about it, because you were too caring a person to make such a far-reaching decision after much thought. I am going to find it very difficult on August 12 this year, remembering that on that day last year, you died.

John's baby arrived, as we all anticipated, on the day your father returned from Abu Dhabi; in fact, just two hours before the plane touched down. It was a girl, Stephen, and they are calling her Rachael. Had it been a boy, the name would have been Ryan Stephen. Rachael was actually born on your Great Grandmother's birthday, and she was quite a lady! Strange to think you would have been an uncle! We have been to see her and she looks like a replica of John, except for her eyes which are very much like Paul's and yours; they slant slightly upwards, like your Grandmother's. Your brothers were delighted with her and bought her a very pretty dress; quite a new event to have a girl in the family.

I know how much you would have enjoyed this event in our lives and there were moments of sadness, knowing you could not be there. You will be pleased to know that Andrew gave the baby a beautiful teddy bear, and you know what he was like about his bear collection! He is growing up Stephen, so much, since you went away.

Your father is off for an interview this week for a more permanent job in the Middle East. This time we may be able to accompany him; much depends on whether or not there is a suitable school for Andrew. We are supposed to be moving house the first week in August, so I do not really know what is going to happen now. The summer has been particularly warm this year; so unlike last summer with its cold winds, rain and darkness. Sometimes I feel that if only the weather had been seasonable, you would have made it through your dark patch, but then who am I to say what the future held for you? In my imaginings I see success and happiness, but that may not have been so and you may have been saved from a more horrendous catastrophe.

Other people have no idea just how much effort is going into normal daily living, for all of us. So much energy is being used as we pick up the pieces of our lives to start again, on a new road. Mark is organising his accommodation for the Education Course which starts in September. This will give him the necessary qualification to teach in colleges of higher education where he will be happier. Paul is working very long hours at a job that he is not really very happy about and is seriously thinking of emigrating to New Zealand. Brian seems reasonably contented with his lot and although he does have his low times, he deeply believes he will meet you again, Stephen. Your closest brother, Martin, is a little confused about his future and everyone at home is trying to help him make the first step, without interfering too much. Relatives continue to 'phone us, to ask whether or not he has a job yet. I wish they would realise that he only completed his degree this month and this last year has probably been the most difficult and painful year of his life.

There are times when I want to go up to these people, shake them hard and ask them to imagine the death of one of their children. Of course I do not do that because I know it is beyond the ability to imagine. If they really looked into our faces, they would know that advice is the last thing we require. Why do they insist on jollying us up? We really are doing our best.

All of us have retained our sense of humour and find something to laugh about every day. We are still able to listen to the problems of others and sympathise, but they will insist on giving advice about our future. One day they will understand, I hope, that this was a period when simply living was one of the most difficult things to do, and the only way we could make it was one day at a time.

Andrew helps us enormously in this respect, just by being a child and living each day as though it were his last! He is on holiday and insisted the other morning on being wakened an hour earlier, so that he could get a full eight hours of play-time in!

Today is Paul's birthday; the final day of July and there are now only twelve days to go before the first anniversary of your death. I am finding this last leg so difficult, Stephen. I cannot sleep at night and I am in a terrible state of anxiety. I know what is happening. I am re-living all the events of those final weeks, except that now I know the outcome. Because there is no way of changing anything, I feel like an observer, tied in chains and unable to do anything about the terrible catastrophe which turned our lives into a living nightmare. What happened last year and what is happening now are getting confused in my head because, you see, Stephen, no matter how illogical it may appear to everyone else, there are times when I feel your life could still be saved. Of course it is all totally new to me. It hardly seems a whisper since you were writing out your birthday card to Paul. Twelve days later you were gone. That seems so impossible to me now.

I spoke to God the other day, and for the first time since you died, I told Him I wanted you back and I did not care what He thought about that. I thought about the priest in church last week who said God would give you anything you asked for, so long as you accepted His will. I know he meant well, but he is just a man who can never experience a son's death. If a mother loses a child what would she be praying for, except all other mothers who had lost theirs? Her sad state would not be capable of needing anything but the strength to carry on. Someone told me the other day that I am now at the angry stage of my bereavement. I'm not angry, Stephen, I'm just lost. How does an ordinary mother cope with her child's non-existence? Does anyone ever really prepare her for that? Of course not.

I felt God understood my pain. I was glad I told the truth of the matter instead of pretending that I was managing magnificently to cope with it all. I would be a strange mother indeed if I did not wish you were alive and well. It is no use talking to me about heaven and how wonderful it is there. I don't know anyone who has been there.

I will just pray to God because He does not mind my tears and my outbursts. Most of all I know He accepts my humanity.

August

We have now received a contract to sign away our house and so it should not be long before we are given a final moving date. Much sadness will surround our leaving because we are all clinging on to past memories. It is just another stage in our lives and, as I said before, Stephen, leaving the house will never remove your spirit; we will be carrying that with us wherever we go. I am glad we stayed on here for the year after you died but if we stay much longer there is a danger that I will see the place as some sort of shrine for you and I will never be able to let it go. For me, the next twelve days will be desperately difficult. If I make it to your Anniversary, I feel I will have turned the first corner.

The annual gathering of the family clan took place at my brother's house last Sunday. There was the addition this year of the new baby, Rachael. For the last three or four years, the sun has always shone but on this particular third day in August, the weather could not have been worse. Torrential rain poured down all that day. There was a bad thunderstorm and the sky was very dark. Sadly it reminded me of early August last year, with its heavy rain and keen winds. We have had such beautiful weather over the last months that it seemed a pity this day should have been so bad. We all made the best of it. Baby Rachael was handed around so that everyone could experience holding this new, tiny person.

As the usual family photograph was taken, I thought of you. Along with your brothers, you had not been to this gathering for a couple of years — teenagers usually find family reunions a bit of a bore. However, there was a photograph of you, a couple of years back, playing the inevitable game of football in their very large garden. I remember that day very well and the way you laughed, when you came home, at the thought of how much food was consumed, saying that if anyone invited our family they would need twelve months' preparation for the event!

In spite of the rain, the football game was played and mud-sodden children sat down to the usual barbecue, which had been prepared holding large umbrellas. I know you would have been amused at the way this family of ours ignores adversity.

It is now August 5 and I am beginning to feel very depressed. There was a play on television tonight, which I watched with the rest of the family. I was strangely affected by a woman in the play who, throughout her life, had been a victim of the circumstances in which she lived. She wasn't like me because she seemed to have no real ideas of her own. However, there were odd moments when I identified with her. On occasions, she would stand up and express her feelings strongly, including her confusion about why she felt certain things. Almost immediately after every outburst, she would apologise and return to the compromised position of being manipulated again. The effort of living in this world, which was not really of her making and did not allow her to realise her own identity, proved too much. She died in the end from an overdose.

When the play was over, my eyes focussed on your photograph, which I keep on the mantelpiece. You looked so smart in your dark blazer and school tie. Your hair was lovely, just the right length but thick and full. Half a smile looked back at me and suddenly I felt the whole essence of you. You really were a beautiful person, Stephen, in every way, and in those few seconds I felt the enormous weight of your loss. The emotional feeling was so great that, although I did not cry, silent tears poured in streams from my eyes. No one noticed, as conversation flowed easily back and forth amongst the family. I wiped my face and opened a book, just staring at the words. Someone asked my opinion about something but I ignored them and pretended to be reading. I really could not make the effort to join in, Stephen, I felt so empty. Neither could I say how I felt because there were no words big enough to express my condition.

You remember the letter I said I would write, to be included in the summer edition of the Compassionate Friends newsletter? Well, it arrived the other week and I received a few letters from other parents who had lost their children through suicide. I have written back to them because I know it helps to realise that you are not the only one. The names of their children ring in my ears and in a way make me feel that you are not alone either, Stephen. The knowledge that there were other young people who felt as you did gives me just a little grain of comfort.

It seems such an enormous step for a young person to take their own life that when you are the mother of that child, you really believe for a while that you are the only one to whom it has happened. There is a great desire in the beginning to find someone else who has gone through this traumatic experience. It is an almost desperate searching, as though you have some rare disease for which there is no cure. People around try to comfort you, but you know they are not suffering from the same disease. It is such a relief when you find others afflicted in the same way and still alive. It does not seem to matter what state they are in so long as they are able to tell you that the same thing happened to them. You gain a strange kind of strength from knowing that whatever is wrong with you, it is certainly not unique. It must be like being told you have a malignant growth and then finding out that you haven't. You become one of the many instead of one alone.

The weekend before the first anniversary of your leaving us was so strange and sad. Although I kept mentioning how it was last year, no one talked of any reminders to me. I had the feeling that everyone was thinking about it but no one was saying anything. There was a heavy air of gloom about and it was difficult to know how to get through this time. I went out to attack the grass in the back garden, which had grown way out of control over the past weeks. It was exactly the same as last year and I half-expected you to pop your head around the corner, as you did then, and say "Fancy a cup of tea, Mum?". The smell of the damp earth gave me peace for an hour or so, and as I hacked away at the grass I felt you were not so far away.

The weekend gave way to Monday August 11; your last day with us. I knew this would be the last time I would say "This time last year, he was . . .". It was the kind of day we could not share with each other; each of us remained locked within our own emotions. We all loved you but you meant something different to each of us and so it would have been an intrusion to talk about you now. It has been such a difficult day to get through.

On the 12th, I awoke about 3.15 a.m. which was probably about the time you died. I walked towards the window and looked at the moon shining through. I didn't cry. I just thought of you. There was a moment when I almost tried to re-live your final minutes. Then I remembered that this kind of thinking would only lead to even greater despair. No amount of reviving memories or re-living experiences would prevent the outcome of events which had taken place a year ago. All that happened then and not today. Today was not a day to recall the events which had ended your life, but a day to recall the happy events in your life. You died during one day but you lived eighteen and a half years, and I know you would want us all to remember the eighteen and a half years rather than that one day. It would be the greatest insult to you to concentrate on the one day you failed us, forgetting the eighteen and a half years in which you gave us so much fun and happiness.

At 10 a.m. your father and I attended a Mass we had said for you. I also had the Mass said for all young people who were going through this uncertain period, prior to starting University. We went down to your grave afterwards with some large red carnations. The sun was shining as we weeded the small plot and we talked about how it seemed like twenty years since we brought you here instead of only one. Perhaps when you are in pain, it seems much longer. We arrived back home to a large bouquet of flowers and a letter from another lady who had lost a son called Stephen. The flowers were from my nephew and his family, remembering us during this sad week. He is especially close to me because I was just twelve years old when my sister died in childbirth. He was her baby and my mother brought him into our home and looked after him until he was seven years old. I thought it was wonderful to have a new baby in the house and we shared many lovely times together. He had to leave us when he was seven, to go back to his father. That was a very sad and unhappy time for all of us. In a different kind of way, he knows about loss. The lady who wrote the letter identified with my feelings, offering heartfelt thoughts and encouragement for me on this particular anniversary. Perhaps pain, in the end, brings people closer together.

Well, Stephen, a year has now gone by and I am loth to end this communication with you. Talking to you has given me much pain but it has also allowed me to open up my heart and in the process learn so much about myself and you. I realise that we both did our best with what we had and no more could be asked of either of us. During the time we were part of each other's lives, we shared many beautiful moments. Blake once said "Catch joy as it flies", and we certainly did that. Neither of us could have known, during those happy years, that our time together was to be cut off so sharply.

There is a poem by Dryden which, for me, gives hope without taking away anything I shared with you

> *Happy the man, and happy he alone.*
> *He, who can call today his own:*
> *He who, secure within, can say,*
> *Tomorrow do thy worst, for I have liv'd today.*
> *Be fair, be foul, or rain, or shine,*
> *The joys I have possest, in spite of Fate are mine.*
> *Not Heav'n itself upon the past has power;*
> *But what has been, has been,*
>   *and I have had my hour.*

It was a joy to know you, Stephen. Your departure from this world taught me what love is all about; I didn't really know before then. I hope one day to know you again, in a time and place I am not capable of understanding now. If forgiveness is necessary, I forgive you. I forgive myself too. There will always be a very special place in my heart for *you*, Stephen.

I know God will give me the strength to live each day as joyfully as I am able, in the absence of the son I loved so dearly. Until that other time in that other place,

My love to you always, Stephen.

Mum.